Back to the Basics

A Christian Boot Camp

Christopher Anderson

CROSSBOOKS
PUBLISHING

CrossBooks™
A Division of LifeWay
1663 Liberty Drive
Bloomington, IN 47403
www.crossbooks.com
Phone: 1-866-879-0502

First published by CrossBooks 1/9/2012

ISBN: 978-1-4627-1350-9 (sc)
ISBN: 978-1-4627-1351-6 (e)

Library of Congress Control Number: 2012900424

Printed in the United States of America

This book is printed on acid-free paper.

This book is dedicated to my family, my brothers and sisters in Christ, my fellow Marines, to all those who gave their advice and input for this book and, most importantly, to our Lord and Savior Jesus Christ whom all honor, glory, and praise is due, thank you. I would like to make a special mention to David Scott and Shelley Canuto, my team mates and mentors in spiritual warfare. Also, to Pastor Billy Keller, whom I have grown under and learned from in the ways of Christ, your leadership and guidance throughout my life have helped shape me into the person I am today.

Contents

Introduction

$\mathscr{I}$n a world where excess is the status quo, the opinion of others is the basis of self-confidence, and political correctness is expectation, many believers in Christ are losing touch with their own basic, foundational beliefs. Basic Christian principles are being sacrificed on the altar of appeasement as Church leaders seek to coexist with secularism. There are those who actively speak out against this heretical practice in the Body of Christ, yet so many believers are still being raised under social conformity.

Far too many believers see Sacred Scripture as merely a collection of stories from long ago that do not have much meaning in modern cultures with our advanced technology, reasoning ability, and global understanding of culture. The rising tide of globalism, global religion, global economics, and global community has increasing prominence in the age we are living. Many believers in the Body of Christ are ill-equipped to confront globalism due to their lack of foundation.

Yet despite all of this, those who do have their feet grounded in the Word of God let denominational differences, tradition, and a general sense of religion hinder them from reaching out to those who do not have a very strong foundation in the Christian faith, this too is a travesty. Our congregations are shrinking as believers lose their foundation! We have become so involved with a good presentation that appeals to the senses rather than the heart and to programs rather than the Spirit of God that we have made Church into a spiritual "fast food" stop. This does not build up the Body of Christ but leaves it malnourished with the attrition rate of believers reflects this sad state.

Every day, people turn to psychics, mediums, horoscopes, and tarot card readers to find some sort of guidance in life, looking for a foundation. The Church is the last place they go because they are not being fed and grounded in scripture. Christians are trading a God lead life for the direction of demons.

It is time for the Body of Christ to rise up in the power we have in Jesus Christ and say, "enough is enough". It is time for us to awake from our slumber, renounce the things which are unbiblical in our practices, and take our stand with Christ and not with the world system we are trying to appease.

It is with this understanding that I was instructed to write this book, which contains some foundational beliefs that scripture teaches. It is not an exhaustive set of teachings, but rather a general explanation on which a believer can build, develop, and grow in. As I wrote this book, my prayer was always that it can and will be used to help train and instruct believers in the basic understanding of what it is to be a Christian. As you read this book, I encourage you to look into your own life and see where each subject applies to you. Also, at the beginning of each chapter is a list of scriptures that I used throughout my research, please look those up in your Bible as you go. I am hoping that each subject will cause you, the reader, to form questions which you can take to your spiritual leaders. Please do not take this on face value, but research and question it, that's how we grow in the faith.

May you be richly blessed in the knowledge that you are loved by God, that you are highly favored of the Lord, that you are the apple of His eye, and that you can do all things through Christ who strengthens you! Be strong in the Lord and the power of His might in Jesus Name!

Chapter 1

Salvation and What it means to you

Scriptural references: Genesis 3:1-24, Romans 6, James 1:14-16, John 3:16-17, 1 Peter 1:18-19, Hebrews 9:14, Philippians 4:13, Hebrews 10:10, 14, Romans 5:12-17, 2 Corinthians 5:17-18

Salvation is when a person asks Jesus Christ to forgive them of their sins and to be their Lord and Savior. It is only through Jesus that we can have salvation from our sins and escape the resulting penalty for those sins, which is spiritual death and eternal separation from God in Hell. It is the greatest miracle and the reason for our creation, which is relationship with God.

Humanity is a flawed race, filled with all manner of sin imaginable. Everyday on the news we hear of children being kidnapped, people murdered, robbery, wars, natural disasters, political corruption, and many other terrible things. You might even ask yourself why God allows such evil to exist in the world. This very question has driven some people to atheism, a total disbelief in God or any other religious deity. The truth is found in the book of Genesis in the story

1

of Adam and Eve. Few other individuals throughout history have been looked at more closely than that of Adam and Eve as theirs is the story of our beginnings.

As the Bible tells in the book of Genesis, Adam and Eve are the first people created. They lived in the Garden of Eden, a Heavenly place on earth where they walked and talked with God Himself. No other human being has ever looked at God face to face and lived with the exception of Adam and Eve. In the Garden of Eden were many trees which yielded many types of fruits. Out of all that was created, God forbad the consumption of the fruit of only one tree. In a moment of temptation, Eve ate of that fruit and gave to Adam to eat also. The fruit was known as the Fruit of the Knowledge of Good and Evil, which when eaten would give the eater the knowledge of good and evil. Since Adam and Eve were already immortal, eating this fruit made them like God in that they were immortal and could decipher good and evil. When they ate the fruit they disobeyed God thus bringing sin into the world. The end result of sin is always death so Adam and Eve ushered in an era of sin and death into humanity. God had no choice but to cast Adam and Eve out of the Garden of Eden because sin cannot exist in the presence of God, hence they are the only two human beings who have looked at God and lived. From that moment on, all humanity, from Adam until today, are born into sin. It took the sacrifice of God's only begotten Son, Jesus, to bridge that gap between God and mankind.

Jesus was born in Bethlehem. His birth, life, death, resurrection, and His future Kingdom on Earth are all prophesied throughout the Old Testament. It took nothing less than a perfect sacrifice to settle the sin debt that we owe God. Since we are all born into sin, we rightly deserve death and separation from God, but you see that is not what God wants. God sent Jesus to be the perfect sacrifice for us so that through Jesus we can have a relationship with Him again. It is this end result of intimate relationship which drove God to wrap Himself in flesh to die for His creation.

Once a person accepts Jesus Christ into their hearts and lives as their Lord and Savior, the penalty of death and the debt we rightly owe God is paid in full. At that point, we can begin to fulfill our purpose, which is to have a relationship with our Creator. As a Christian, you now have access to God through Jesus to fellowship with Him and to share your life with Him. No longer are you bound by the sin that you were born into, but you are free to live a life of purpose and meaning. A person's life becomes full because the hole in our lives created by our sin nature is filled with God's mercy, grace, and love as His children.

Through your life by your example, people still in sin can witness the goodness of the Lord. The liberation that I am sure you feel is evident to those who are not saved and are still in their sin. You are living proof of God, Jesus, and the Holy Spirit. The best part of it is that it is all a free gift that God gave you, not because you deserved it but because God loves you and has shown you His grace and mercy. Within ourselves we have to ability to only temporarily change who or what we are but it's only through Jesus and the working of the Holy Spirit that we can experience lasting change in our lives. The constant development we undergo throughout our entire lives as Christians, with all our mistakes and successes but still being set apart for God is known as sanctification. Sanctification means set apart. Believers have been separated from their sins and set apart to God by the once-for-all sacrifice of Christ. As long as we are on this earth, we will make mistakes. When we mess up the Holy Spirit will let us know by pricking our conscience. Then is when we need to ask for forgiveness again and try not to make the same mistake twice. However, the reality of things is that we will more than likely mess up again at some point until eventually whatever it is that we have been messing up we will no longer do. Sanctification is also the continual, ongoing process by which believers are being made more and more perfect. Christians are in a continual state of sanctification, being set apart for God and being made perfect through all of our ups and downs, twists and turns. As stated before, we learn through our mistakes. Christ's death perfects us, the sanctified.

Many times, people say that they felt this great, euphoric moment when they were saved while others question their salvation because they did not experience that same euphoria. Yet we must not mistake our own personal feelings and emotions with what is written in God's Word. When I gave my heart to God in January 1993, there was not a great euphoria that accompanied my confession of faith. At times, I even questioned why I didn't feel that emotion until I realized that being a Christian is not about the emotions and feeling, but about what God's Word says. Did I confess with my mouth the Lord Jesus Christ, believe in my heart I am forgiven through His sacrifice, and confess my sins? Yes, I did do that, so though there was no great euphoria, the fact remains that I was saved all those years ago. If you are reading this now and you can say that you were the same as me, rest assured that your salvation is secure. The only time to call this into question is if you just said the words with no intention in turning from sin and in complete unbelief. Remember, actions are the results of thought and intent.

At this point I would like to emphasize that we all mess up. It is a fact that at some point you will sin again. The media is always searching for big name evangelists who commit fraud, fornicate, embezzle church funds, or whose tempers tend to flare up at one point or another. As long as you live you are going to have the potential to mess up. Don't get frustrated at yourself when you fall. Learn from your mistakes, that is how you grow. Don't concentrate your thoughts to when you did something wrong, that is how we stay down when we fall. Don't worry about messing up again in the future, the more you fall the more apt you are to watch where you go which will eventually result in less falling and more walking the way we are intended to. Always remember that there are people out there who have stumbled where you may have stumbled. These people are a great source of knowledge and wisdom in your time of struggle. They can relate to you, they know how to pray for you and encourage you, and they know the feelings of failure you might experience as a result of falling down. This is another reason why Christians are a family of brothers and sisters. Remember that every family has its internal strife and fighting. Expect to see this. Unfortunately, the meaning of salvation has been mixed in with church politics and hierarchy. Salvation is all about freedom in the Spirit, the promise of eternal life through Jesus Christ, and relationship with the Father. No other miracle you may witness throughout your life is as great as salvation because the soul of a person has been saved from Hell. You are evidence of the greatest miracle, a person saved by God's grace through your faith in Jesus Christ.

Chapter 2

Baptism and its Significance

Scripture References: 2 Timothy 3:16-17, Luke 23:40-43, Acts 2:38-41, Acts 8:26-40, Matthew 3:3, Matthew 3:5-6, Matthew 3:13-15

There are two main ideas as to the significance of baptism held in the Protestant Church today. One idea is that baptism is a requirement for salvation and the other is that baptism is not a requirement for salvation. There are scriptures that back up the root of each idea so in order to get to the bottom of this debate we must look throughout the Bible and analyze baptism based on the circumstances of the individuals written about therein. This is a hot topic among the different denominations and is a source of disunity in the church. As a Christian, you will be faced with many different debates between denominations therefore it is important to have a Biblical foundation to base your ideology during these times of question. The will of God is written in His Word, which is the Bible. All scripture is the inspired word of the Living God given to man through the Holy Spirit.

Baptism was a ritual used by the Jews as a picture of cleansing and purification. Gentiles, or people other than Jews, who converted to Judaism would dip themselves in water as a sign of being cleansed from their old life. This was, and remains, the initial act of worship for anybody converted into Judaism. Before entering into the temple, Jews would dip themselves in water to show their desire for purification. These ancient baptism pools can still be seen at the base of the temple mount underneath the Muslim quarter in Jerusalem. Even today, Gentiles that convert to Judaism have to be dipped in water to show cleansing from their former life. In the Christian faith, this tradition lives on as a sign of the passing of life lived in sin to life lived for Christ. It is an outward display, showing the world physically what has taken place spiritually. Baptism serves as confirmation from the new believer that he indeed is a new creature, born into the body of Christ.

John the Baptist is a well known figure in the New Testament whose ministry was to call the people to repentance in preparation for the arrival of Jesus Christ and His ministry. John's call was for repentance of sin followed by the Jewish ritual of cleansing to demonstrate outwardly the repentance of those he baptized. Though Jesus was without sin, He went to John for baptism in order to fulfill the will of God, confirm John's ministry, and to join with the believing remnant of Israel. In following the example of Jesus, we should be baptized as it fulfills the will of God and demonstrates our unity with Christ.

Throughout the letters of Paul to the various churches and in the book of Acts, which is the follow-on book to the Gospel of Luke, the topic of baptism is addressed and demonstrated through actions. In Peter's sermon after the fall of the Holy Spirit on Pentecost, he makes the proclamation, "repent and be baptized for the remission of sins". On that day, three thousand people repented of their sins, accepted Jesus Christ as Lord, and were baptized into a new life. In Philip's ministering to an Ethiopian on the road from Jerusalem, the Ethiopian asked Philip what hinders him from being baptized, or showing his desire for purity through ritual washing. Philip's response was simply, "if you believe with all your heart, you may." At this the Ethiopian responded that he believed in Jesus as the Son of God and his Savior and they immediately stopped for Philip to baptize the Ethiopian. The defining theme here is that believing in Jesus and repenting of your sins is the means of salvation followed by baptism as the outward expression of the desire to be pure. Baptism is in line with the word of God, or the will of God, and being baptized is obedience to God.

The Gospel of Luke records an interaction between Jesus and the two thieves that He was crucified with. One of the thieves ridiculed Christ and mocked Him while the other rebuked that thief, requesting Jesus to only remember him when He enters into His Kingdom. At this display of faith, Jesus responded by saying to the thief that he would be with Him in paradise. As we already know from chapter one, salvation is only through belief in Jesus. The comment made by the thief recognized Jesus as the Son of God when the thief declared Jesus entering into His Kingdom. That simple statement held in it this man's hope of salvation in Jesus. Though this man died without having been baptized, he entered into the Kingdom of Heaven because of his belief in Jesus Christ as the Son of God. If only the other thief had accepted Jesus as his Savior as well he would not be in Hell today. This situation dictated the necessity of baptism therefore we can see through this event that baptism is not required for salvation.

Another often discussed topic of baptism is whether or not there is a time laps required from the time a person repents and they are baptized. In the first century church, people were baptized immediately following their conversion. There was not a set time limit in between conversion and baptism. As the centuries progressed and pagan rituals and ideology infected the Church, a period of three years was set between initial conversion and baptism. This time period was for indoctrination in the faith and for the Church leaders to determine whether or not a person could truly live a perfect life before permitting baptism. There is no Biblical grounding for a period of time between initial conversion and baptism. Unfortunately, many of the Church traditions and practices still have their roots in pagan practice rather than the Word of God. Two thousand years of compromise is hard to eliminate. Each time that baptism is mentioned in scripture, it is immediately following repentance. There was no standard of perfection that a person had to attain in order to be baptized nor was their any indoctrination. After all, it is not up to us to judge whether or not a person has sincerely accepted the Lord as Savior or not. As His will is "that none should perish but that all should come to repentance," we are to merely speak the Gospel message of salvation to all. From there we are to grow in God's Word and to minister to others in the faith for mutual growth and nourishment. That is what this book is all about, growth, nourishment, and the spreading of the Gospel message.

I remember growing up and seeing all kinds of methods that people were baptized. My step father, James Rison, baptized people in a back woods creek. While I was in Afghanistan, a Corporal gave his heart to the Lord and was baptized in a water filled bucket of a bulldozer because there was no baptismal on the base. I have even heard of people being baptized in a water filled feeding troth. Even if there is no official baptismal in a Church building, we recognize that water baptism is a symbolic ceremony representing the death of our former, sinful life and the resurrection of a new life lived in Christ Jesus. It is the blood of Christ which covers our sins and makes us new. Water baptism symbolized in the physical body the washing by blood in the spiritual body.

To summarize this chapter, baptism is ordained by God as an act of worship to Him for all those who believe and receive Christ as their Savior. As such, we are to be baptized in the name of the Father, Son, and Holy Spirit in accordance with God's will. Nonetheless, in extreme circumstances such as a person on their death bed or in a situation where it is impossible to be baptized, salvation rests solely on the profession of faith that Jesus is Lord, having asked Him to cleanse the individual of their sins and turning away from sin.

Chapter 3

Christian Living

Scripture References: Matthew 7:17-20, James 4:7-10, Galatians 5:22-26, 1 Corinthians 10:13, 1 Corinthians 2:9, Romans 12:9-21, 1 Peter 1:16, John 14:15, Matthew 25:14-30, 1 Peter 4:7-11, Colossians 3:12-17

The Christian lifestyle is imaged by the world as one of strict rules, condemnation for violating the standards of perfection imposed by the Ten Commandments and worldly thinking, and of being "holier than thou" in attitude. However, contrary to popular worldly belief, Christians are free. We are not weak as some people tend to imagine, but strong and full of life. There is no condemnation for one who has been liberated through salvation in Jesus. The reality of Christian living is that a person who is a child of God always has the Holy Spirit directing their path, even when they make a mistake. There is hope, joy, love, peace, and security in the wonders of the Lord's grace and mercy. There is no fear of death or man, only the proper reverence of God. We have confidence in our confession of faith and our testimony, always striving to serve the Lord however we can. There is nothing that we cannot do through Jesus Christ in the power of the Holy Spirit.

The Christian lifestyle is one all can freely enjoy but that few choose to live. The example that we show those around us can be a most powerful tool in ministry. The trademark signature of a faithful Christian is seen through the fruits that they bear, both in words and in action. No experience on earth can compare to being a child of the one who carved out the Grand Canyon, who rose up the Rocky Mountains, who filled the oceans with life, and whose awesome grace holds the planets in orbit. Being able to have a relationship with the Master of the Universe is the most exciting journey that anyone could ever embark on.

The name Christian means "one who belongs to Christ". In the New Testament, this term for followers of Christ only appears in three places. Church members did not have a distinctive name in the early days, instead they referred to themselves as "brother and sister", "disciples", "believers", "followers of the Way", or "saints". Christian was first used as a word of contempt against the saints in Antioch. Jews called believers "Nazarenes" instead of Christians as Jesus was from Nazareth, a city which the Jews saw being evil as a result of the Roman occupation at the time. Again, the term reflected contempt towards believers. The first converts to the Christian faith were from Jewish origin. As the Apostles spread the Gospel throughout the region, many more Jews came to the faith. With Paul's ministry specifically directed toward the Gentiles, more and more converted from paganism to Christianity. Antioch was a major city in which Paul ministered, resulting in many more converts. It was the neighboring communities of Antioch who began to refer to the saints in Antioch by their new name, Christians.

Throughout history, Christians have been persecuted for their belief in Jesus and their adherence to His word. Many have been put to death for their confession. From the first martyr, Stephen in the book of Acts, Christians have been killed because they refuse to recant from their beliefs. All who have died for their faith and who continue to die are living examples of the Christian lifestyle, living because they are alive with Christ. Many accounts recall condemned Christians singing praises to God in the hour of their death, others ministering the Gospel to their executioners, some embracing the crosses they were crucified on and the stakes they were burned alive on, and some who requested more intense and sure deaths than prescribed. All meet the Lord with smiles on their faces, joy in their suffering, and forgiveness in their hearts towards their enemies. They all considered what they had in this world as loss. Their actions speak volumes today as Christians are still persecuted and murdered for their faith. Despite many attempts to kill off Christians, eliminate the Bible from existence, and destroy all symbols of Christianity, the faith continues to grow beyond its trials.

The truth of the Gospel has revealed the imperfection and filthiness of this world whereby causing very hostile reactions from those who are in sin. Many people that you love may reject you for your faith in Jesus. Some people will hate you and go out of their way to make your life hard. During those times, know that your trials and tribulation are not in vain. As long as there is sin in the world Christians will go through trials and tribulations. Through the three and a half years of Jesus' ministry, many religious leaders of the time plotted and made attempts to kill Him. If Jesus suffered persecution, then we will too. We are by no means greater than Christ, therefore if He suffered, we will suffer too as His servants. Hold fast to your confession of faith in Jesus and rest in the knowledge that Jesus is with you every step of the way through your own personal trials and tribulations.

As a Marine, there are many aspects of life that I have faced which do not confront the typical civilian who has never served. Military service in general confronts a believer with unique challenges in their Christian life. I have been asked many times why it is that I do not use profanity. One reason is that, to me, profanity shows a lack of education. If a person cannot express themselves without using profanity, clearly there is a lack of linguistic ability or understanding. Second, I want to be different than everyone else because I am called to be separate from them. Third, I feel that profanity is not appropriate. Of course, these are my personal opinions. We, as Christians, have to base our actions on scripture. We also must remember that we are called to be separate from the world.

Christians have been described in the Bible in many different ways. From soldiers, farmers, athletes, workers, vessels, and fishers of men to salt, light, branches, stewards, ambassadors, priests, and sojourners. The Christian lifestyle is one with many comparisons all of which emphasis a portion of life. But there are different characteristic traits that a Christian posses. Giving tends to be among the more predominate traits. Giving money, buying someone a meal, giving clothes to the needy, giving of time, and giving help with no regards to receiving in return are all examples of the giving nature of a Christian. Humility is a trait that tends to take some time to develop, especially in American Christians, but once developed is a distinguishing trait seen in Christians. The Fruits of the Spirit, as described in Galatians 5:22-26, are other traits that you know a Christian by. Jesus said that we will know them by the fruits that they bear. If someone's life is lived contrary to the Word of God, they do not belong to Christ. If someone lives in accordance to scripture, they are in Christ.

We are called to be in the world but not of the world. This statement basically means that we are to be separated to God, or sanctified, and live life accordingly. We are to be holy as God is holy. There exists a fine line between living life satisfying your own pleasures and fulfilling the desires of God in your life. You will notice that your own desires begin to mirror that of God's desires for you. When viewed in the original Greek, we are to be in the world, or planet, yet be separated from this age, or the world's system, which is the domain of Satan as he is the god of this age. The world's system is one which perpetuates fleshly sin in our lives by making access to these sinful desires much more available. For example, adultery, lust, and fornication are enhanced by the world in the form of pornographic materials and overriding sexual themes on television and in the movies. Lying is also another example of the corruption of Biblical standards by the world's system. The world says it is okay to say a little white lie as long as it doesn't hurt anybody yet God says that he hates liars. There are many other ways that the world corrupts God's Word and rebels against His Divine system which I will discuss in another chapter.

As a people free from the bondage of sin through the acceptance of Jesus as our Savior, we are presented with the choice to serve God or not. When we were sinners, we did not serve God because we were enslaved to our sin. There was no liberty to choose who we served; we sinned because we couldn't help ourselves. If you have ever tried to quit smoking on your own, you know what I am talking about. The desire to quit is there but the means to accomplish that goal is not because of nicotine's addiction. Very few people are able to quit cold turkey. A vast majority of people need quit smoking aids in order to stop their addiction. The same is true with sin. We cannot be free without Jesus. Since a Christian is free from the bondage of sin, we have to choose each day whether we will live that day for God or whether we will live for ourselves. God never forces us to do what is right. He loves us and does not force us to love Him because true love is never forced. If we love God, we will follow His instruction. This is our free will which God never violates. The choice is yours each and every day until you die.

When it is all said and done, how we lived our lived here on earth will determine our reward in Heaven. Different rewards will be given based on our works while we are here on earth. Being faithful to your calling as a Christian sets you up for a greater Heavenly reward. Our life here is only preparation for eternity in the Lord's service in Heaven. The gifts and talents that God gives us here, when used in service of the Kingdom of Heaven, will be rewarded both here and in eternity as good stewards and servants of the Lord.

The parable Jesus gives in Matthew 25:14-30 of the faithful servants applies in this manner as well. Christians are the servants of God, in whom Jesus has given abilities, talents, and gifts. With these, we are to sow them into the works of God, whether it is using a talent for music to glorify God, your naturally joyful demeanor to lift up others, your ability to speak for spreading the Gospel message, or any other gift, talent, or ability to further advance the Kingdom of Heaven. We can all attest that there are some people that seem to have it all, yet we must realize that God gives to all according to their ability. God knows our mental, emotional, and physical limits and only gives us those things which do not exceed our abilities. Just as the unfaithful servant with one talent went and hid his talent, Christians must be weary of failing to use what God has given to us. Not using what we have is like burying our gift in the ground, like the unfaithful servant did with his one talent. If you notice at the end of this parable, the unfaithful servant's gift was given to the one with ten talents and that servant was removed from the master's presence and thrown into outer darkness where there is weeping and gnashing of teeth. This is a stern warning from the Lord Himself to use what we have been given and not waste our abilities. The reward comes in increase of our abilities and a harvest for the Lord in our earthly realm and we are put in charge of other things and enter the Master's joy in the Heavenly realm. The gift of salvation and the other talents, gifts, and abilities we are given from God is meant for sharing with others that everyone can grow in God.

Many times your greatest enemy will be your flesh, which is a way of saying your old self. When we are saved, our old self is crucified and we are made into a new being in Christ. We are in a constant struggle within ourselves to mortify our old self so that the new life can reign within us. Therein lies the grace, mercy, and love of God in that He knows the old self will rise up at times but He is more than willing to extend His forgiveness when that happens. This is the choice we have to make everyday, to walk in our old self or to walk like the new creature we were made into when we received Jesus as Lord. Christians at times tend to give the devil too much credit for the situations we find ourselves in. We reap what we sow; there will always be consequences for our actions, whether good or bad. When you find yourself in a bad situation, take a step back and see if you put yourself there because of letting your old self have its way. Maybe then you'll find that it is you who is your greatest hindrance in your Christian walk. That is where you mature and grow in Christ. The Holy Spirit directs our path and the Word of God teaches us how to walk in it, but it is our choice to walk.

No matter what situation we may face, no matter how severe the conflict internally or externally, no matter the numbers against us, we must choose to fight and rely on God for our help, as Jesus promised us a Comforter, a Helper, and Power in the Holy Spirit. Every aspect of life presents us the opportunity to choose Christ or ourselves. Every idol thought, every careless word, every flagrant act, every missed opportunity, and every division, all stemmed from a decision made from the conscious mind or from a conditioned response. Our bad habits, compulsions, and thoughts must be subject to the unfailing truth of the Word of God. The only way for a Christian to be subject to the Truth of God is through meditation and memorization of scripture, a devoted prayer life, regular fasting, and regular attendance in a congregation of believers of like faith. These are the tools Christians use to conform to scripture.

Fasting is traditionally viewed as refraining from eating or drinking while spending the time one would usually eat and drink in prayer. Though this is true, fasting can also be other things, such as not watching TV, surfing the internet, gym time, or some other activity that you enjoy. A fast is a sacrifice from yourself when you deny your fleshly body something it wants in order to seek God. We discipline our bodies in this manner.

Prayer is our "telephone line" to God as it is our communication with Him. As stated before, a relationship with little to no communication cannot develop but decays. When we pray, we relieve whatever burden's us at the time by placing it on Jesus. Jesus says in Matthew 11:28-29, "Come to Me, all you who labor and are heavy laden, and I will give you rest. Take My yoke upon you and learn from Me, for I am gentle and lowly in heart, and you will find rest for your souls". Through prayer, we can take everything that weighs us down, the burdens that cause us to labor under the load, and give it to Jesus. He promises to give us rest. Prayer has the ability to calm our minds, to refocus us on the task at hand.

Scripture memorization and meditation is tremendously important. The Word of God is our sword we use to battle our flesh, the world's system or age, and the devil. If we have not memorized scripture, we may be confronted in a place where a Bible is not available and the Word is not planted in our heart and mind. Many times, my own personal meditations on scripture has opened up scripture in many different ways which have helped me recover from my battles in the spirit as well as giving me new ways to fight. I will dive deeper into this in a later chapter.

Lastly, regular attendance in a congregation of like minded believers. This is also a drastically important aspect of the Christian lifestyle. When we are surrounded by like minded believers, we have a support group and experience far beyond anything the world can offer. Church leaders are there to mentor you and to develop you into a strong man or woman of God. Their insight and leadership is invaluable in your walk with Christ. I like to think of going to church as a first aid station. This is the place we come to for healing, rest, restoration, strengthening, support, and hope. The battles we engage in throughout the week can be very destructive and devastating, but when we attend church, we are treated for those wounds. I cannot stress enough attending church. Pastor Jesse Duplantis said it this way in his sermon, Close Encounters with the God Kind, "I don't miss church. It is a divine appointment with God. It is a service for me." This attitude begins to touch on the holiness and sacred duty we have as Christians to go to church and be in the presence of God with fellow believers.

"Love must be without hypocrisy. Detest evil; cling to what is good. Show family affection to one another with brotherly love. Outdo one another in showing honor. Do no lack diligence; be fervent in spirit; serve the Lord. Rejoice in hope; be patient in affliction; be persistent in prayer. Share with the saints in their needs; pursue hospitality. Bless those who persecute you; bless and do not curse. Rejoice with those who rejoice; weep with those who weep. Be in agreement with one another. Do not be proud; instead, associate with the humble. Do not repay anyone evil for evil. Try to do what is honorable in everyone's eyes. If possible, on your part, live at peace with everyone. Friends, do not avenge yourselves; instead, leave room for His wrath. For it is written, **Vengeance belongs to Me; I will repay,** says the Lord. But **if your enemy is hungry, feed him. If he is thirsty, give him something to drink. For in so doing you will heap fiery coals on his head.** Do not be conquered by evil, but conquer evil with good" –Romans 12:9-21 HCSB

"Therefore, God's chosen ones, holy and loved, put on heartfelt compassion, kindness, humility, gentleness, and patience, accepting one another and forgiving one another if anyone has a complaint against another. Just as the Lord has forgiven you, so also you must forgive. Above all, put on love-the perfect bond of unity. And let the peace of the Messiah, to which you were also called in one body, control your hearts. Be thankful. Let the message about the Messiah dwell richly among you, teaching and admonishing one another in all wisdom, and singing psalms, hymns, and spiritual songs, with gratitude in your hearts to God. And whatever you do, in word or in deed, do everything in the name of the Lord Jesus, giving thanks to God the Father through Him." –Colossians 3:13 HCSB

Chapter 4

Heaven and Hell, Angels and Demons

<u>Scripture References:</u> 66:1, Psalms 11:14, Ecclesiastes 5:2, Luke 15:7, Revelation 4:9-11, Revelation 22:1-5, John 14:2, James 1:17, Revelation 21:4

$\mathcal{T}$he question of life after death is as a predominate concern for many individuals. People want to know that they will live on in one way or the other when they die. Accordingly, if there is life after death, there must be a God. Good and evil, God and the devil, Heaven and Hell, angels and demons. They are all opposing forces that exist in a constant state of opposition in order to have a balanced universe or so goes the world's theory. Many people claim to have been to Heaven or Hell when they had a near death experience. God has given visions to people throughout history of Heaven and Hell as well as of Himself. Even the devil appears to people thorough various means. People have seen angels and demons and have been influenced by them at times. I have been and I am sure that you have been at some point. We will trace through scripture Heaven and Hell and what angels and demons are and their influence in our lives as Christians.

Heaven is the place where God dwells. Heaven also is a reference to the sky so it is important to be able to distinguish between the two in scripture. When Heaven is used to describe the place where God dwells or where people who are saved go to when they die, this is the place. Scriptures referring to where birds fly, gathering of clouds, rain fall, etc., this is in regards to the sky we all see when we look up. The Bible also refers to space as heaven as well. Paul mentions being caught up to the third Heaven, which is referring to the final destination for believers.

Heaven is the place where the righteous go when they die to live forever in the presence of God. Within Heaven are streets of gold, rivers, trees, magnificent beauty, and no darkness. There is not even a shadow, for "God is light in whom there is neither darkness nor shadow of turning". There is no sun, for God is its source of light. It is a place of pure love, not defiled by the sin of this world. We even have our own mansion in Heaven. No need is ever left unmet and no want is ever left empty. Heaven is a place of service where we will continue to minister to all those in Heaven with us. This is part of the importance of working in the ministry that God has given to us here on earth, as it is practice for things to come. There will be no more tears, no more pain, and no more death as we will forever abide in the presence of the Almighty. Worship and praise are continual in Heaven as we give our all to God. If you are a shy person that finds it uncomfortable to clap during the worship service, raise your hands in the air in surrender to God, or to pray loud enough for someone next to you to hear, you will be brought out of your shell in Heaven for sure. Eternal life starts with belief in Jesus, but eternity starts in Heaven.

On the complete opposite spectrum are the horrors and terrors that exist in Hell. This is an existence that is beyond any horror ever experienced on earth. As Heaven is the dwelling place of God and the redeemed, Hell is where sinners go when they die. Unfortunately, many people choose to reject God's plan of salvation through His Son Jesus. They send themselves to Hell for rejecting Christ and the salvation that He freely offers. Hell is the consequence of denying Christ as Lord and Savior. People reject Christ by not believing in Him or simply by the very sinful nature they are born into. Our choice is Heaven or Hell, belief in Jesus and trusting Him or not. It is this individual choice which recognizes our allegiance with or against Christ.

Hell was created for the devil and his angels, or demons, and was never intended for humanity. When Satan decided to ascend the Throne of God, he sinned and was removed from his position in Heaven and made to cross between Heaven and earth. Hell was created to punish the devil and all the fallen angels who rebelled with Satan. As God's creation, Satan decided to cause humanity to fall by convincing Adam and Eve to disobey God. This is how the devil attempts to get back at God, by taking as many people to Hell as he can. Through sin, Satan enslaved humanity. Freedom came when Jesus died and rose from the dead. This is when humanity was given the choice to accept Jesus as the Messiah and be liberated or to continue to live in slavery to sin.

Hell is eternal punishment for the rejection of Christ and a life lived in sin. It is the wrath of God on all sinners. God is a righteous judge who judges based on perfection. As all have sinned through Adam, nobody can meet God's standard and are judged accordingly. Through Jesus, we meet that standard as we are redeemed through His blood and being sanctified and made pure through His sacrifice if we choose to follow Him and trust Him. Those without Christ are eternally in the wrath of God in Hell. Darkness so black you can feel it, fire so hot that it sucks all of the oxygen from the atmosphere, screams of the damned so loud and full of terror, putrid smells of burning flesh and all manners of stench, hunger and thirst that never goes away, demons ripping you apart yet you stay in tact, hopelessness so complete that there is no thought of escape, your senses heightened that you feel, smell, see, hear, and taste all the horrors to their fullest. These are a vain attempt to describe the torments of Hell that await sinners. The flesh is eaten from the inside out by worms as you are burned in a blazing inferno for all eternity. Though everyone in Hell begs and pleads for death, death never comes as it is a reprieve from punishment and a source of hope. Constant memories of life on earth and the rejection of Christ run through the thoughts of the damned. The knowledge that they put themselves there by rejecting Jesus plagues their every moment. Though surrounded by people, they are completely and utterly alone in their torment. There is no hope for communication with anyone as the only voices heard are cries of pain and sorrow. Nothing good exists in Hell. No food, no fresh air, no friendships, no water, no peace, no sleep, no nice scents, and no hope. These are only some of the things we can enjoy on an earth which is corrupted with sin though in God's grace, that are absent in Hell. There are no parties or reunions in Hell as people tend to think, only horror and torment forever. Hell is a place to avoid at all costs.

God created everything, including Heaven and Hell as well as angels. Everything created has a purpose. Ours is to have a relationship with God. The devil himself started out as an angel of the Lord, one of the most beautiful ever created with the purpose of ministering to God through music and his beauty. Those angels who rebelled with Satan, who was known as Lucifer prior to his fall, also had a purpose in their creation. All forsook their proper domains as angels and became enemies of God. Though Satan wants to be a god, he cannot. He can only be in one place at one time, which is why fallen angels, or demons, have to help spread darkness and evil throughout the earth. Originally, these demons and the devil were not evil and served God in Heaven as part of the angelic host. Through Satan's pride and the resulting rebellion of the angels, they became evil against their created purpose. Just as humanity chooses now to serve the Lord, the angels choose too. There is no redemption for fallen angels like there is for humans. Once they fall, they are forever at war with the saints of God and with the Lord. This is how angels become demons and how the devil began his evil attempt to destroy mankind.

Angels have many different purposes. They impact our lives in various ways. The Heavenly Host, as angels are sometimes known as, serve God through ministering to us, bringing revelations and messages to humanity, interpreting visions and dreams, and through engaging in warfare. One of the most well known angels is Michael the archangel. Michael is one of the chief princes and a leader of the Heavenly Hosts. He is a mighty angelic warrior. Gabriel is also a well known angel who brings messages and revelations to mankind. Gabriel interpreted Daniel's visions, announced John the Baptist's birth as well as the birth of Christ, and he stands in the presence of God. The word host comes from a verb meaning "to fight" or "to serve". Hosts are appropriate for angels because they serve God and they fight, as evident through the workings of Michael and Gabriel, the archangels. Angels are at work in our lives when we pray against the works of the kingdom of darkness. They come as answers to our prayers by fighting demonic spirits in the spiritual realm as was the case with Daniel. Angels are a great source of help in our walk with Christ.

When I was a kid, my family took a trip to Kmart to purchase a tread mill for my mother. James, my step father, was taking the shopping cart back into the store after loading the car. On his way out, he saw a homeless man sitting on the bench struggling to put on his socks. This man was filthy and had infected sores all over his feet and legs, yet with the most beautiful blue eyes James had ever seen. The man, filthy and putrid smelling, asked James to help him with his socks. Three times the man asked and three times James could not because of the condition of the man. On the third request, James gave the man some money. At this, the man said with love and peace in his eyes and voice, that it was ok. The crushing weight James felt accompanied him to the car and we drove around the parking lot looking for the man so we could help him with his socks. This homeless man, who could barely walk, had vanished in a matter of a minute. James then had the realization that he had encountered and angel of the Lord. He had been praying for a long time prior to this encounter for this kind of event. Yet, even though the encounter did not yield helping the man with his sock, the spiritual lesson was beyond any monetary amount that could have been given. We never know when we may encounter an angel of the Lord in our daily interactions. Hebrews 13:2 states "be not forgetful to entertain strangers, for whereby some have entertained angels unaware." I learned from James' experience as well. As a result, I have become more aware of my interactions.

Demons are fallen angels who assist Satan in spreading evil and darkness throughout the world. They are agents of the kingdom of darkness, also known as the kingdom of this world. Demons pose as false gods, like Baal, Ashturoth, Beelzebub, Moloch, Merodach, and Baal-poer. These were all gods served by the Canaanites, Phoenicians, Babylonians, and other pagan people. These false gods required human sacrifice to be satisfied. Parents would throw their own children into raging infernos, toss their children from high walls, and drain their blood in acts of worship to these false deities. Demons have domains which they rule. Abandon, or Apollyon, is the demon of the bottomless pit. Leviathan is the demon of the sea. In the book of Daniel, demons also were in charge of nations, like Persia. Demons influence the lives of people through temptation and even can possess the bodies of people and influence a person's thoughts and actions. They recognize believers and the power they have through the Holy Spirit to cast them out. Demons seek to steal, to kill, and to destroy all that is holy. Demonic forces actively engage all believers through bringing doubt and fear so that the believer will not fulfill the works of God in their lives. Demons bring sickness and disease to inflict humanity. Temptation is the main weapon that demons use against humanity.

When I was stationed in Washington State, the Lord told me one day to tell all those who work with me that He loves them. I hesitated at first and tried to rationalize with the Lord that they all knew that, yet He told me to do it anyway. So, in my own way I went up to each person in my work area and said, "Hey man. You know the Lord was talking to me and told me to tell you He loves you, so Jesus loves you, man." The typical response was first, surprise, then acceptance of the message, and then they would go about their business. One particular individual displayed a much different reaction. This man always seemed to vehemently oppose any type of religious speech. Every time I tried to tell him about the Lord, he would get so angry. As I approached him with the same sentence that I used with the others, his expression turned to sheer hate and anger. Then I saw it in his eyes, a presence that was alien from the man I work with. I smiled at it and went back to my work. After a few seconds, I looked up and to my surprise I saw what appeared to be a black mass in the shape of a bear like creature climbing up the wall. Its mass was made up of what appeared to be a swarm of insects that made the outline of a huge, bear like figure. A few seconds later, it disappeared then the man I had just talked to seemed to become himself again.

Yet another experience I have had involving demons occurred when I was a teenager. At the time, I listened to bands like Marilyn Manson, Cradle of Filth, Dimmu Borger, and Emperor. For those of you who do not know, these bands sing about Satan, demonic worship, and various occult topics. Though I was saved at the time, I got into these bands because of the musical content, not the lyrical. Yet it was the lyrics that were the most destructive to me spiritually. My step brother was also beginning to get into the mystical world of magic, like is seen in the Harry Potter films and many cartoons at the time. There was also in his family a warlock. However the demon gained access, whether through the music I was listening to or through witchcraft, I do not know, but a demon came into our home.

We both lived in two room additions that were in the attic. I would feel it's presence in the corner of my room by the attic door and see black figures out of the corner of my eye. I would wake up at times with deep scratches all over my upper body. This thing even pushed me down the stairs one morning. I never knew that my step brother had any issues until one night; he woke me up with terrible screams. Of course, being the teenager that I was, I yelled at him to go back to sleep. After well over an hour of this screaming, I got upset, threw open the door to his room and flipped on the lights only to see him in the corner of the bed, sitting up with the blankets up to his chin in this wide eyed look of pure terror across his face. I asked him what was going on and he told me that there was a black figure in his room with red, glowing eyes that was standing on the opposite side of the room staring at him. He said that when I turned on the light, it slowly melted down into the floor. I ran, grabbed my Bible, and began reading scripture in his room. After a little while, I left and went back to bed, keeping his light on. Later on, we told my step dad what had happened. While we were at school, he went into the attic rooms and cast out the demon. Afterward, he anointed the window seals and door frames with oil. We never had another issue with that demon after he did that. Little did we know that other family members claimed the pet bird we had was smacked off its perch across the cage during the same period of time the demon was in our rooms, so the demon was all over the house.

Christians without the knowledge of their authority and power over the kingdom of darkness tend to have more difficulty in dealing with demonic attacks in their lives. Some Christians are even afraid of the possibility of confronting demonic spirits. We can rest in the fact that we have not been given a spirit of fear but of love and a sound mind. Christians have been given the authority through Christ to tread on scorpions and serpents, which are demons. We are mighty warriors in Christ Jesus, a fact which I will expand upon in a later chapter. Even in the rebellious teenage years, I knew that the Bible was the sword that I needed to use to fight. Though I didn't know how to use it properly to fight, my step dad did.

Angels and demons are not metaphors that we use to teach spiritual lessons or to describe the inherent positive and negative nature of humanity. They are real spirits with real implications in our lives. Where angels are sent to minister to us, deliver messages, fight in the spiritual realm, and help us at times, demons are there to steal, kill, and destroy us.

Heaven and Hell are not metaphors used to describe aspects of life. We are not living in Hell here on earth because of all the bad things that happen. Heaven and Hell are very real places that the eternal spirit of a person goes to when they die our certain natural death. We have the choice, do we believe in Jesus Christ and accept the free gift of salvation He offers us through His blood or do we not. We choose Heaven or Hell while we live.

Chapter 5

The Holy Spirit and His Role in Our Lives

<u>Scripture References:</u> John 3:3-5, Romans 8:11, 1 John 2:20&27, Acts 2:17-41, John 16:13, Micah 3:8, Romans 15:16, 2 Thessalonians 2:13, Romans 8:16, Hebrews 10:15, John 14:16-26, Romans 14:17, 1 Corinthians 2:10-16, 1 John 4:1-6, Galatians 5:22-23, 1 Corinthians 12:3-11, Acts 9:31, 1 Corinthians 2:12-13, Ephesians 1:16-17, Isaiah 40:13-14, 1 Corinthians 2:10-13, Acts 2:39, Acts 1:8, John 20:22-23, Acts 2:1-4, Matthew 10:34, Romans 8:36

The Holy Spirit is apart of the Godhead also called the Trinity. Just as Jesus is God yet separate from God, so the Holy Spirit is God yet separate than God. They are all different in their roles yet they are all God. The three are one yet they are three. This is a spiritual mystery that we may never understand completely until we are in Heaven. The Holy Spirit is the fulfillment of the promise Jesus made concerning the comforter He would send so that His children wouldn't be alone. He is also the creative aspect of the Godhead, the One who makes things happen.

After Jesus rose from the dead, He was seen for forty days ministering to His disciples. During that forty day ministry, Jesus commissioned His disciples to go into the world spreading the gospel. He breathed on them and they received the Holy Spirit. Though they believed that Jesus was the Messiah promised by God, it was not until Jesus died and rose again that they were able to have eternal life. When Jesus breathed on His disciples, they became born again. All of the disciples were Jews. Though they all followed Jesus throughout His earthly ministry, the disciples still had to accept Jesus' sacrifice on the cross. Once the disciples were born again, they received the Holy Spirit into their lives the same as all who come to salvation through Jesus. This indwelling of the Spirit is only confirmation of the salvation a person accepts. It is the Holy Spirit who bears witness of our salvation.

Throughout our lives, we are made aware of our mess ups when the Lord speaks to our conscience. The feeling of guilt that we have when we sin is the Lord speaking to us. The Holy Spirit convicts us of the wrong things that we do. He is the one who draws us to salvation through our conscience, making us aware of when we sin and birthing in us the need of a Savior. Just like the disciples, when we ask Jesus into our lives as Lord and Savior, the Holy Spirit confirms the salvation we've accepted. He continues to convict us of our sin from that point on whenever we mess up and He never brings back the conviction of past sins we've repented of. This is only the beginning stages of the working of the Holy Spirit in our lives.

Jesus tells His disciples that they will receive power when the Holy Spirit comes upon them in the book of Acts. The day of Pentecost was when all those in the upper room received that power. All who were in the upper room were gathered together in one mind and in one accord waiting on the promise of the Holy Spirit and power that Jesus made before he ascended to the right hand of God. As they were gathered, the sound of a mighty rushing wind filled the upper room and tongues like a flame of fire was seen above their heads. They all began to speak in other languages the oracles of God. The people outside heard the commotion and came to investigate the noise they heard. Each person who came to see what was going on was from all parts of the world, with many different languages. Each person heard those in the upper room speaking in their own native language. All the people present were in Jerusalem for Pentecost, which was a Jewish ceremony ordered by God through Moses in the Old Testament. As they gathered from outside, some began to ridicule those in the upper room as being drunk while others saw the event as an act of God. At the confusion, Peter stood up and began ministering about Jesus and the promised Holy Spirit that they now had. That day, three thousand people accepted Jesus as Lord, were baptized, and received the Holy Spirit. This was the power that came, through the disciples the Holy Spirit would convict the lost and draw them to Jesus. Other power through the Holy Spirit followed. Healing the sick, casting out demons, not being hurt by poison, discerning hearts and other gifts followed as well. As Christians, we have the same ability through the empowerment of the Holy Spirit. We have to pray for this empowerment through the Holy Spirit. Simple confirmation from the Holy Spirit that we receive when we accept Jesus as our Savior is different than the power we see here with those gathered in the upper room. We must pray for this empowerment just as the disciples did on Pentecost. Every born again believer has the right to this power but few are those who seek God for Holy Spirit empowerment. Just like the choice to accept Jesus as Savior and living life according to scripture is a willful decision we make, praying to God and seeking Him for empowerment through the Holy Spirit is a choice we all have to make.

When I lived in Washington State, I served in the music and youth ministries. We had a number of evangelists and missionaries who fellowshipped there. One day, the Holy Spirit spoke into my spirit to approach one of these missionaries and speak to him Jeremiah 33:3, which says "Call on Me and I will show you great and mighty things, which you do not know." I was thinking to myself when the Spirit instructed me to speak, "Lord, this man is a missionary and an elder in the church, he knows this." Nonetheless, I did as I was instructed. As my brother in Christ heard what I was instructed to speak, it was as if a burden had been lifted from his shoulders. He was so grateful for the word and, after we talked for a while, I left feeling just as blessed as he did. You see, often times we question what the Lord is instructing us to do, yet we do not know the situation of the other person's life which requires the words we are instructed to speak. The best thing to do is speak what God has told you to speak. Just know that God will never go against His word, which is scripture, so if something you feel to say is against scripture, keep it to yourself because that is not from God.

The Holy Spirit gives the believer unnatural boldness. It took boldness to speak what the Lord instructed me to an elder and missionary in the church. May times throughout the Letters of Paul, Paul and the other disciples were persecuted for their faith, even in the face of death. Yet throughout their ordeals, all held true to their faith without ever wavering. The gospel was presented to royalty, murderers, religious leaders, and others who would not hesitate to kill anyone who preached the doctrine of Jesus Christ. Christians in modern times also have this type of boldness, especially in countries like Pakistan, China, and Vietnam where Christianity is outlawed and those practicing the faith are sent to prison and executed for being followers of Christ. Jesus promised us that He came to bring the sword and not peace. As long as sin is in the world, their will always be a battle between those who are saved and those who are lost. The Holy Spirit helps us throughout our time on earth with boldness to proclaim the gospel of Jesus Christ in the face of persecution, imprisonment, and even death. Even in America, there is an increasing distain for believers. There is quickly coming a time when even American Christians will be forced to worship in secret as the church buildings will become a target for those who desire the end of the faith. Stand strong and know that through the Holy Spirit you will overcome, for we are more than conquerors through Christ. Later, I will discuss the Gifts of the Spirit.

Chapter 6

Jesus and His Miracles

Scripture References: Joshua 10, Matthew 14:22-33, Matthew 8:28-34, John 3:16-17, Hebrews 4:15, 2 Corinthians 5:21, Mark 4:35-41, Mark 1:23-28, Mark 7:24-30, Mark 9:14-29, Mark 5:1-20, John 15:13

Jesus Christ is the Messiah, the Son of the Living God. He was crucified and rose from the dead three days later. He ministered on earth for forty days following His resurrection before ascending to the right hand of God where He is now interceding on our behalf before God. He was God in the flesh when He walked on earth two thousand years ago. He was tempted in every way that we are now yet He never gave into temptation nor sinned. Jesus knows the struggles that we go through and sympathizes with us in every way; therefore He is the perfect representative of the human race before the Throne of God. Throughout His earthly ministry, Jesus gave proof of His deity through various signs and wonders. All four Gospels bear witness to the miracles Jesus performed, some Gospels more than others. Entire books are written detailing every miracle and sign Jesus performed as well as His life and how it fulfills Old Testament prophecy. This chapter will be an overview into some of His miracles and a highlight of a select few in establishing how certain wonders in themselves proclaim Christ's deity.

Miracles are documented throughout the Old Testament and the New Testament but all pale in comparison to Jesus' miracles in both frequency and scale. With three words, "Lazarus, come forth!" Jesus raised Lazarus from the dead! By speaking the word, Jesus healed the centurion's servant without ever coming to the centurion's house. People born with birth defects, like withered limbs, blindness, deaf and dumb, all came to Jesus for healing and He healed them all according to their faith. With a single command, Jesus calmed the raging storm. Demonic spirits trembled when Jesus came near, they begged and pleaded with Him and they worshipped Him. No other Biblical figure ever demonstrated such power and authority. Most importantly, Jesus forgave sins. He continues to work miracles today through the gift of Salvation that He offers.

By calming the raging sea, Jesus demonstrated His authority over nature itself. The disciples marveled at this and wondered what manner of man Jesus was because even the winds and the waves obeyed His voice. Though the storm was fierce around the disciples and their boat, Jesus slept. The disciples lacked faith that God would see them through the storm, as it was exceedingly violent. Yet the whole time, the One who created the world was there with them in their storm. When they called on Jesus to help them and save their lives Jesus sent forth the Word and nature obeyed its Creator. It wasn't a matter of Jesus crying out to God because He is God in the flesh. His creation, nature, recognized its Creator and obeyed His voice and became calm and peaceful. When Joshua commanded the sun to stand still until Israel had revenge on their enemies, he had to cry out to God whereas Jesus did not. That which is created is never greater than the Creator.

After this display of authority over nature, Jesus defied the laws of gravity by walking on water. When Jesus went up into the mountain by himself to pray, He commanded His disciples to take a boat to the other side of the sea. Early the next morning, while sitting in the middle of another storm at sea, the disciples saw Jesus walking to them on the water. At the sight of this, they feared that He was a ghost. Jesus called to them and told them that it was Him and not to fear. When Jesus climbed aboard the boat, His disciples worshipped Him and declared that He was surly the Son of God. Even natural laws are subject to the One who created the laws and have to follow after what God is doing.

Multiple times people who were possessed with demonic spirits received deliverance when Jesus came near. Those in opposition to God recognized Jesus' deity by confessing Him as the Son of God when addressing Him. Many times the demons begged not to be tormented by the Lord and pleaded to not be destroyed by Him. When Jesus commanded them to leave, all departed, even the legion of demons in one person. In the presence of God no sin can exist, therefore in the presence of Jesus demons must flee or face annihilation. The enemies of God all recognize God and tremble at His presence, all rebellion and dissention must take place away from the Lord but must conform to Him in His presence.

The greatest miracle of all is the forgiveness of sins. Even the religious leaders of the day proclaimed that only God can forgive sins when they saw Jesus forgiving people of their sins. No matter how many people He healed, how many demons fled from before Him, or how often He defied nature, if Jesus never forgave sins or died on the cross for the remission of sins we would all still be sinners. Those healed would still go to hell healed sinners. By forgiving sin, Jesus establishes the foundations of a relationship with Him. From the fall of Adam and Eve in the Garden of Eden until Jesus died and rose again, God desired to restore His relationship with humanity. Since the foundations of this world, God knew that He would come to mankind in the flesh and die so that relationship could be restored and we could have fellowship with Him again. There is no other act of love greater than laying down your own life for a friend. This love was and is demonstrated when people are reconciled to God through accepting Jesus as their Savior and receiving the free gift of Salvation. You, the reader, are a walking example of the greatest miracle of Jesus and of the love of God toward his creation, humanity.

The four Gospels record only a specific number of cases in detail of the various miracles and healings that Jesus performed. Yet, many times, it is simply written that as many who came to Him were healed. The Gospel of John states that there are not enough books in the world to contain all that Jesus performed. With this in mind, Jesus tells us in John 14:12, "most assuredly I say to you, he who believes in Me, the works that I do he will do also; and greater works than these he will do, because I go to My Father."

Chapter 7

Who Jesus Said He Was

Scripture References: Hebrews 13:5, John 10:10, 1 Corinthians 2:9, Matthew 7:15-20, John 6:35,41,48,51, John 8:12, John 10:7,9, John 10:11,14, John 11:25, John 14:6, John 15:1,5

Throughout our lives we come into contact with people who we do not know. Only by talking to one another and sharing who we are with one another are we able to establish a relationship with that stranger who then becomes a friend. All relationships stem from a basic understanding of who the other person is by their testimony of themselves and the words of others who know that person. For example, I am a United States Marine, a musician, a son, a brother, an uncle, and a veteran. Those describe me to a degree to a certain audience. My characteristic traits also describe who I am, things like friendly, loving, caring, easily approachable, and understanding. Even so, you have certain traits by which you would identify yourself to someone else. The same is true with Jesus. His life and death was detailed in the Old Testament through various prophets as well as

His ministry and His future Kingdom on earth after the Great Tribulation. Looking at who Jesus said He was is just as important in understanding Christ. Knowing Jesus through His words about Himself also can open doors to understanding who He is in our lives as Christians. We can begin to recognize His handy work in our surroundings, in our hearts, and in our spirits. This will also become the catalyst for a deeper relationship with Jesus, which is His desire for us. As you read through this chapter, take the time and reflect on your life up to this point and see if you can identify where Jesus has been. This might be difficult at first but eventually you will be able to see more and more places where the Lord has intervened on your behalf in one way or another. As His favor towards you sinks in you will begin to realize that He has never neither left you nor forsaken you, even when you were at your worst, Jesus was and is always there with you.

In the Gospel of John, Jesus uses seven "I Am" statements to describe who He is. These statements are both statements of character and relation. These seven describe Jesus' nature and relation because they describe how His character relates to us. That, in and of itself, is a clear example of how God wants to be an active part of our everyday lives. Who He is encompasses His longing to have a relationship with us.

In the first of the seven "I Am" statements, Jesus says that He is the bread of life. Just as bread sustains physical life so Christ offers Himself to us to sustain our spiritual life. As we are all born into a world of sin we are spiritually starving. In order to have eternal life we must be nourished by the Bread of Life. All who are without this spiritual nourishment are destined to die. Just as malnourished people die a physical death so do people who are malnourished in the spirit die a spiritual death, which is Hell. Jesus meets our needs for nourishment so that He may have a relationship with us and so that we may have spiritual life in Heaven.

Jesus says that He is the light of the world. We have all woken from a nightmare in the middle of the night. The first thing we do is reach for the light switch to make sure that nothing is there to hurt us. We need that light to calm our fears and reassure us of our safety. In a world where everything is dark with sin, Jesus offers Himself as a light to guide us. He reassures us of our safety in Him. Light itself is a symbol of holiness, therefore in Christ we are made holy. Without Christ, we live in uncertainty and fear. With Christ we can be assured of our faith and be optimistic about our future. As we let the Light guide us through life, we are sure of our place. We have a purpose and a mission in life, both which will be illuminated by the Light.

The third statement Jesus makes about Himself is that He is the door of the sheep. This statement is understood by those who are shepherds but not so well understood by others. For protection, shepherds guided their flocks into stone enclosures at night. These enclosures did not have doors so the shepherd would stay at the opening throughout the night to fend off any attacks on the sheep by predators as they slept. This statement describes Jesus' care and devotion to those who are His, Christians. The Lord fights our battles. Though we may be surrounded on every side by those who would do us harm, Jesus Christ is there to fight for us. What better protection than to have the God who created the universe on our side.

The forth statement follows the third as Jesus calls Himself the good shepherd. Just as those who are hired to watch over the flock of sheep at night might run when danger approaches, Jesus remains committed to our defense and safety. His care and devotion to us is more than any other imposter shepherd. Many false religions out there seem good in the good times but when things begin to go bad for a person there misplaced faith fails them and they are devoured. We can have everything this world has to offer but if we do not have Jesus in our lives everything will fail us. Nothing in life is as certain as Jesus. A good example of this is Job, in the Old Testament. Though Job lost everything, God still protected him and sustained his life. So too will God sustain your life in the worst of situations.

Jesus is the resurrection and the life. He is the Lord of all life and has the power to raise the dead, even Himself. For those who are in Christ, death is not the final word. Though our physical bodies die in the natural, our spirit will live forever with Him in Heaven. Those without Jesus die both in the natural and in the spiritual as they will abide forever in Hell. Jesus is the source of all life; in Him we have life in abundance. What we call waste God calls abundance. When it looks like we are overflowing with blessings, it is Jesus demonstrating His love through abundance in our lives. We cannot fathom the abundant life that God has prepared for us.

Lastly, Jesus says that He is the true vine. The Old Testament contains references to Israel as God's vine. Due to the nation's unfruitfulness, Jesus came to fulfill God's plan. By attaching ourselves to Jesus, we enable His life to flow in and through us. Then we cannot help but to produce fruit that honors the Father. We are likened unto branches attached to the vine that produces fruits. These fruits are the good and acceptable workings of our faith through the fruits of the spirit. We are known by the fruits that we bear. If our vine is Jesus our works will be good and in line with the Word but if our vine is not Christ, our works will look a lot like the world. We are called to be separate from the world, to be in the world but not of the world. If Christ is the vine to our branch then we will be able to live a life holy unto God apart from the sin that runs rampant all around us. Therefore, through Christ we are able to be sanctified, or set apart, to God. Then we can pursue a deeper relationship with God that is beyond anything we can imagine.

Through these seven characteristic traits of Christ from His own words, we are able to view God's desire to be our constant companion. Some people tend to shy away from becoming a born again Christian because they do not want to give up the pleasures of their life. Things like partying (being drunk, smoking dope, ect.), being promiscuous, and mistreating others to make themselves feel good seem to be what people want to hold onto so tightly. If people knew the things that God has in store for those who love Him they would put off their fleshly, worldly desires for what God has.

Every person has a choice in life to live for God or for their own pleasures. There are many other aspects and traits about God that Jesus did not so clearly specify but are written throughout the Bible that show who God is. There is no better friend and no greater enemy than the One who thought up humanity and created us so perfectly. Nothing else will ever fill the void a person has in their lives like God can. Even as Christians, we have to choose everyday to life for God or for ourselves. Just as we need food everyday to keep us going, so we need the Bread of Life to sustain us. We must be connected to the True Vine to bear witness to God's goodness. Our protection lies in the Good Shepherd. Our bearing everyday will be skewed if we walk without the Light. We need Jesus in our lives as much as he needs to be apart of us.

Chapter 8

How to Pray

Scripture References: Matthew 6:9-15, 1 Kings 19:11-18, Mark 11:25-26, Mark 11:22-24, Matthew 7:7-12, Acts 9:1-19, Exodus 3:1-22, John 10:1-5

Every relationship that a person embarks on depends on communication to flourish and grow. At the end of the day, for example, a husband and wife share with each other how their day went. This communication is important to maintain a healthy relationship with each other. The same principles that we follow in any human relationship also applies to how we are to share our lives with God. We communicate with God through prayer, reading our Bibles, and worshiping Him. We should be frequently communicating with God, just as we would with our spouses, best friends, or our parents. Before we can discover how to pray, it is important to understand what prayer is and how daily prayer strengthens our relationship with God.

Prayer is a means of communication with God. It is our "phone line" to the Throne of the Almighty. Through prayer, we touch God. By prayer, we can inquire of the Lord, or ask something of the Lord. But more than simply a means to an end, prayer is also a spiritual weapon. The power of prayer lies in the fact that you are petitioning the Lord God for intercession in a given situation. In these cases, the person praying is referred to as an intercessor. Jesus Himself said that whatever we ask in prayer, believing and not doubting shall have whatever we ask. There is power in prayer with the combination of faith and action in our faith. When we pray, trusting Jesus to do what He said He would do is the key.

Jesus, when asked how to pray, gave us the model prayer. Many people can quote this prayer and probably have heard it recited verbatim on different occasions. Matthew 6:9-13 contains the Model Prayer that Jesus instructed His disciples:

"Our Father in Heaven, Hallowed by thy Name, thy Kingdom come, thy will be done on earth as it is in Heaven. Give us this day our daily bread and forgive us our debts as we forgive our debtors. Lead us not into temptation but deliver us from the evil one. For Yours is the Kingdom and the power and the glory forever. Amen."

This prayer can be broken down into five sections, each of which illustrates how to pray. With the understanding of how to pray, as instructed by Jesus, your prayer life will begin to take on a new form as your faith grows. Prayer will not be just another "religious" thing to do but a welcomed appointment with God. As your prayers begin to be answered, you'll even find yourself praying without noticing.

The first part of the Model Prayer, or the Lord's Prayer as it is sometimes referred to, is the greeting and exaltation of God. The phrase "Hallowed be thy name" is another way of saying may Your name be hallowed, or holy. Therefore, Jesus was illustrating that God, whom is addressed, is holy.

When we honor God as holy and lift up His name as such, we are worshipping God. Our opening prayer then is an act of worship before interceding for others or asking things for ourselves.

The next part of the prayer is the denial of our own ambitions and expectations in favor of the Lord's will. "Your Kingdom come, Your will be done, on earth as it is in Heaven" is how we die to our fleshly goals and submit to God. This is a proclamation of the spread of God's Kingdom on earth and the fulfillment of His will throughout the planet as well as in our lives. Here is where the person praying acknowledges that God's will reigns supreme over their lives and they are subject to His voice. Our ambitions and expectations are laid down and we accept God's will for our lives.

"Give us this day our daily bread and forgive us our debts as we forgive our debtors." This is the body of the prayer. Here is where the one praying asks of the Lord for whatever they need. Daily bread is a representation of being sustained. All that we need to live is provided by God. This point is also where the prayer can take on the form of intercession. Confession of our sins before God is one of the most important parts of our prayer life because sin separates us from God. We are all still flesh and we all make mistakes. It is imperative to ask God to forgive us of those sins whenever we pray so that our prayers may be heard by God. Jesus lays on us the stipulation in the follow on verses to the Model Prayer that if we do not forgive others of their sins against us that God will not forgive our sins against Him. By harboring unforgiveness in our hearts towards others, we will be held accountable of our sins before God. Search your own heart each time that you pray. If there is someone in your life that you need to forgive or ask forgiveness of, do so before you pray so that your prayers will be heard by God. If you don't, your prayers will not be heard by God because your life is stained and reeking of sin.

The forth part of the Model Prayer is a plea to the Lord for His continual protection. "And lead us not into temptation but deliver us from the evil one." God does not tempt us but instead guides us from temptations. With temptation comes the prospect of a potential downfall. The person praying should ask God to keep them from being snared by temptation. For example, a recovering alcoholic would be tempted every time they pass by the local bar. In order to avoid that temptation, the individual would all together avoid the bar. Social drinkers on the other hand might have to avoid certain peer groups to avoid that temptation. Pornography is an addiction held by many people throughout the world. To avoid that temptation, a person might have to disconnect their internet, avoid the video rental store and magazine stand. God does not put those temptations before us but instead can lead us away from them through pricking our conscience, providing a means to avoid certain places or people, or by filling the time with wholesome activities. We are also liberated from the evil one when we avoid things that tempt us to sin. Satan and his demons use temptation as their weapon against us. The devil and our own fleshly desires are continually trying to draw us away from God, especially through our addictions. God protects us by leading us around temptation and warning us of points of downfall. If we stumble and fall, the Lord is full of grace and mercy to forgive us of our mistakes and He will continue to guide us away from temptation if we just listen to His voice.

The last part of the Model Prayer is again an exaltation of God's majesty. "For Yours is the Kingdom and the power and the glory forever. Amen" This is a declaration that all things belong to the Lord and whether or not He answers your prayers right then and there or whether He answers them later or not at all, you trust in His wisdom and power. This, too, is an act of worship in that you humble yourself and lift up God. Don't forget, God moves in His timing, which is very different than ours. We must simply trust that God will do what His Word declares He will do. Remember, God cannot lie but must be faithful to what He says.

When put all together, your prayers take on a new identity with substance and power beyond what you may realize. A prayer should be worship, denial of self and acknowledgment of God's will, confession of your sins and inquiry/intercession, plea for continual protection, and worship of God in closing.

Hearing back from God is an exciting moment in anybodies prayer life as it is a faith builder. God speaks to us through our conscience, through other brothers and sisters in Christ, and through His Word. These three are some of the more common ways that God speaks to us. In order to hear God's voice in any method He chooses to communicate back, we have to learn to quiet our hearts and minds. God spoke to Elijah in a still, small voice, not through extravagant methods, though some people need a dramatic display of God to heed His voice. God sometimes answers prayers through visions, much like the vision that Paul had of Jesus on the road to Damascus. The Bible has many different examples of how the Lord speaks to His people. One of the most famous illustrations is of Moses and the burning bush in the Book of Exodus. God spoke to Moses through the flames of the bush, though the bush was not consumed with the fire. However the Lord decides to speak to you, having a clear heart and mind is the key to hearing Him speak. Jesus said that His sheep know His voice and that they follow Him. You will know that God has spoken to you when He speaks. Your heart will know it.

So many people get so frustrated when they do not hear back from God when they think He should respond to them, especially in a crisis situation. What we have to realize and understand is that God's timing is not our own. Peter says in 2 Peter 3:9 "the Lord is not slack concerning His promises, as some count slackness…" Here, Peter is mentioning salvation yet this also applies to every aspect of life. God has His time for everything and that timing is not based on us as individuals. Daniel, when we prayed and fasted for 21 days, continued to press into God until he received his answer from the angel of the Lord. That angel was sent because God heard Daniel's prayer on the first day, yet the angel had to fight through demonic forces to reach Daniel. Had Daniel been like most Christians of today and gave up after only a few days, he would have never received the answer he was looking for.

Nothing has changed in the spiritual realm from the time of Daniel till now with the exception of salvation through Jesus. The same battles rage in the heavenly realm. We have been commissioned by Jesus after He rose from the dead and before He ascended into Heaven to cast out demons and heal the sick as found in Mark 16:17-18. These things occur when we pray, fast, and seek God's face instead of His hand.

Many people, when they pray, are only after what blesses them at the moment. God is a good God and will give us the desires of our hearts, yet there is so much more reward in seeking God's face instead of His hand. Jesus said to seek first the Kingdom of God and His righteousness and everything else will be added to you. David, in the Book of

Psalms, said "I have never seen the righteous forsaken nor his seed begging bread". We must seek God's face when praying, to know Him and His ways.

Jesus speaks to His disciples in Luke 11:5-8 about persistence. He asks them who would go to a friend's house late at night and ask for bread. Though the friend is in bed with his family and the house is closed up and locked, it is the persistent knocking that will cause the homeowner to answer. Of course, the homeowner gives the bread and whatever else would be needed. The same is true with God. When we are persistent in our prayers, we know that God will provide abundantly beyond all we may ask or think.

Faith is the key to unlocking the blessings of the Lord in our lives. We will see creative miracles, the dead raised to life, demons fleeing, and people healed of their sicknesses when we have faith. Faith is simply trusting Jesus to do what He said He will do and giving up our sense of timing for when we think He should move. When we trust Jesus completely, allow Him to do the work He said He would do, and realize that it is not our own righteousness but Christ's righteousness in us, we will see hospitals emptied, morgues going out of business, and a revival of the likes we have never witnessed before. We have to lose the instant gratification mindset which has infected our society over the last few decades and simply let God be God.

We should pray daily as a means to build our relationship with God. He is waiting on you to talk to Him and be His blessing. Just as we can bless our husbands and wives by telling them about our day, we bless God when we tell Him about our day. Having somebody care enough about you to talk to you about their good times and their bad times is a blessing in that we are trusted and liked by someone else. We show God that we trust Him and care about Him when we pray and when we listen to what He says. Take some time before reading on to the next chapter and pray. Tell God about your day, He already knows how it went but He still would like to hear about it from you. You'll feel much better when you do if you're having a rough day today. Remember, Jesus is not only our Savior and Lord, but also the closest friend we will ever know. He relates to us because He is both perfectly human and perfectly God!

Chapter 9

Spiritual Gifts and You

Scripture References: 1 Corinthians 12, 13, 14, 1 Peter 4:10-12, Romans 12:6-8

Growing up as a child, there was nothing more exciting to me than getting up before the sunrise on Christmas day with my brothers and sisters, waking my parents up and opening presents. Oh, there was so much excitement and joy with every piece of wrapping paper that I tore through. Year after year, I would dive right into all my gifts all at once! Then, my parents got the idea to hand out the presents one at a time, one person at a time, so that we could all enjoy watching each other opening up gifts. That first year with this new Christmas tradition was nearly unbearable! Nonetheless, towards the end of the pile of gifts, my parents gave in and I got to go at my presents like I did in years past. Even now, though I am a bit older and wiser, I am still filled with excitement every time I get to open a present.

God gives us gifts too and these gifts are things which only He gives. Just like at Christmas with our family, these gifts are given freely, not because we have done anything to deserve them, but because we are loved by God! His presents are much better than money can buy, more precious than gold and silver, and they help others too. There is no lump of coal if we were bad at one point or the other either.

The original Greek translation of the English word spiritual gift is "pneumatikos charisma". Charisma is a word that we hear in our culture to depict a person's charm or attractiveness that inspires devotion in other people. Yet in Greek, charisma means "that which is graciously given" or "favor given". This is important in understanding and accepting gifts from God. Pneumatikos means "the spiritual things". When these two words are put together, they literally mean in English "the spiritual things which is graciously or favorably given". Just as a child is given gifts from their parents at Christmas or on their birthday out of their parent's love, so our Father, God, gives us spiritual gifts because He loves us! We are all His children if we have accepted Jesus as our Lord and Savior! He has favor towards His children! His grace is new every morning towards us, just as it is written in Lamentations 3:23.

God gives to each of us one or more gifts for the benefit of the entire Body of Christ. As we each belong to a particular congregation of believers where we live, those spiritual gifts that we have been given are to be exercised and used to build up the congregation that we belong to.

Just as the human body is made up of many different parts with many different functions, so too is the Body of Christ made up of many different parts with many different functions. Not every part of the body is used to see; how could we hear, smell, taste, and touch if every part were an eye? Our thumb holds just as much importance to the entire body as does the hand, which the thumb is a part of. The same holds true for the Body of Christ and the congregation that you belong to. Each spiritual gift that God gives to His children holds just as much importance to the congregation of believers they fellowship with. Though their roles may be less important than others, though some receive more honor than others, though some have more glory than others, each spiritual gift is an essential part to the edification of the whole. A congregation without one or more of these spiritual gifts in operation is like a body that has multiple amputations; it is not whole and does not function the way it was intended. A believer who does not exercise their spiritual gift can in a sense cripple the overall function of the congregation they belong to.

God gives spiritual gifts to all of His children according to His will. He also gives these gifts to us when we seek them through prayer, petition, and communion with Him. The gifts that our Father gives are: words of wisdom, words of knowledge, great faith, gift of healing, working of miracles, prophecy, discerning of spirits, different tongues, and the interpretation of tongues. With all of these gifts, the greatest is love.

Love is kind, longsuffering, doesn't envy, does not parade itself, is not puffed up, is not rude, is not self-seeking, is not provoked, thinks no evil, does not rejoice in iniquity and sin but rejoices in the truth, bears all things, believes all things, hopes in all things, endures all things, and never fails. Though a person may give prophecies , work miracles, heal the sick, cast out demons, speak in tongues, or be able to know the mysteries of God, if they do not have love, these gifts lose their meanings. 1 John 4:8 says that God is love, therefore to have love is to have God and to know Him. By loving others, we are expressing God to them. Speaking in tongues will end, prophecy will fail, but love never fails.

There exists a hierarchy of spiritual gifts in the Church. In order, they are apostles, prophets, teachers, miracle workers, healers, helps, administration, and variety of tongues. An apostle is someone who is sent out as a messenger. Prophets are those who serve as the middleman between God and humanity. They deliver messages that God gives them to a congregation. Teachers are those who instruct in scripture and can be the pastor or Sunday school teacher. Miracle workers are those who pray for others and God instantly restores them. Healers are those who pray for others and gradual restoration of the body occurs. The difference between miracles and healing is miracles are instantaneous and healings are gradual. Helps can be anything that helps maintain the Church building, strengthen or support the ministry teams, or people who cook a meal for a visiting evangelist. Administration is just that, managing things like money, phone calls, maintaining a Church website, or putting together the weekly Church bulletins. Tongues are last because they edify the individual speaking rather than helping the entire body. Only when there is an interpretation of tongues is it edification of the body but when there is no interpretation, tongues should remain a personal time of prayer and communion between the one speaking and God.

Though every gift is important, there is a special emphasis in 1 Corinthians on prophecy, love and tongues. Love is the greatest gift, as I have already shown. Paul instructs us to pursue love and desire spiritual gifts, but especially the gift of prophecy. Prophecy is a gift that is intended for the edification of the Church and is for believers. God uses His prophets to communicate with His people. Isaiah, Daniel, Ezekiel, Elijah, and Elisha are some of the Old Testament prophets who brought the children of Israel great revelations from God concerning their future, the future of the world, and foretold of the coming Messiah, who is Christ Jesus. These men of God also told of the sure and swift judgment of God if the people did not change their ways and turn back to God. Today, prophets are used by God in the same way. They warn us of judgment, of the future, and of the soon return of Christ. As awesome a gift as prophecy is, love remains greater than prophecy.

Tongues can be the language of angels, as Paul is referring to, or it can be speaking a foreign language that a person does not know. For instance, if a person from Egypt is in the congregation, a person with the gift of tongues may begin speaking the things of God in Arabic, though they have never learned nor studies the Arabic language. The gift of tongues is for nonbelievers when it is interpreted and its interpretation can also edify the congregation. Tongues must remain personal when there is not interpretation. This is the lesser of the gift because it is intended for nonbelievers with interpretation and for the individual believer speaking in tongues without interpretation. Some denominations place a huge emphasis on speaking in tongues as it is evidence of what is known as the baptism of the Holy Spirit. This is evidence that the Holy Spirit is working in a person, but the Holy Spirit comes to reside in the believer when they give their hearts to God the moment they are saved. The gifts of the spirit are empowerment for the service of God as seen in Acts 1:8. Speaking in tongues is a spiritual gift but the emphasis needs to be on the gift of prophecy and love more so than the gift of tongues according to Paul in 1 Corinthians 14:1-5.

Many mainstream denominations teach that the Holy Spirit does not work the way He did when scripture was written in the 1st Century Church. These denominations do not have the full function and mobility in their congregation because they are crippled by unbelief, false doctrine, and tradition. Human nature is to discredit and discount anything that we have not personally experienced or have personal knowledge of. People, regardless of their theological ideology, like to pick and choose what they want to believe and not believe scripturally. The gifts of the spirit are frequently thrown out. For a Christian who does not operate in their spiritual gift or who do not believe they can have a gift when they ask for it from God, they are not living like the new creatures they were intended to be. Stifling the gifts God has given them has handicapped their potential as a believer and crippled the congregation the believer belongs to. Everything in scripture, from Genesis 1:1 to Revelations 22:21 is the inspired Word of God, the God who is the same yesterday, today and forever, who never changes, who keeps His promises, and who never lies. Everything in scripture is truth and one hundred percent reliable, even those things which we do not fully understand, comprehend, or what causes us guilt and discomfort. We must always maintain this understanding and base our entire lives, in thought and action, on the infallible and unwavering truth of the Word of God.

As you read this, you may already know what your spiritual gifts are that God has given you. If this is the case, I encourage you to use your gifts for the edification of the congregation that you belong to so that the Kingdom of God can be furthered in your community. If you have not received a spiritual gift just yet, seek God and ask for the gift that He wills for you to have and operate in.

Chapter 10

Understanding the Church as the Body of Christ

<u>References:</u> John 17:21, Galatians 5:22-23, Galatians 5:13-15, James 2:14-26, Romans 10:9-10, Matthew 16:16-19, Ephesians 4:14, Romans 12:1-2

The word church has come to mean a place where people of like faith gather on designated days of the week to worship God. It is used to define a person's denomination and style of worship as well as to establish social groupings. Our generation also uses church outside of Christianity in other worship systems, such as the Church of Scientology and the Church of Satan. Once again, the implications are more of a social nature. Interestingly, due to the social classifications within the Christian world as well as with the non believing world, the word has largely been divorced from its original meaning as intended by Jesus and Paul.

Church, when used with a capitol 'C', is used to describe the entire body of believers regardless of denomination. As a believer in Christ, you are the Church. Just as we are called to be "in the world but not of the world", we are separated from all others as Christians, or the Church. This term is the collective of believers, known as the Body of Christ, though more correctly, as the Bride of Christ. Jesus told Peter, "upon this rock I will build my church and the gates of hell will not prevail against it". In Greek, the word Peter means rock, therefore upon the confession of Peter, that Jesus was the Messiah and the Son of God, the church was built. This confession is what makes a person to identify with Christ, the confession that Jesus is Messiah. Paul makes this clear in his letter to the Romans when he said, "If a person confesses with their mouth Christ and believes in his heart that God raised Him up from the dead, he shall be saved". Of course, this initial act of belief in Jesus is followed with baptism, all of which are acts of worship to God. Once a person believes in Christ, the Holy Spirit confirms their salvation by coming to live within them and making them into a new creature through sanctification, which is the ongoing process of becoming like Christ. At once, we become the Church as well as identifying with a church or place of worship, because of our unity in Jesus by faith socially and spiritually.

Within the Church, there are divisions. Catholics and Protestants, Baptists and Pentecostals, Methodists and Lutherans, traditionalists and non traditionalists, they all bring division and disunity within the Body of Christ. In John 17:21, Jesus prayed for the unity of believers, that we will all be one as He and God are one. Today, we see every type and shape of denomination and "Christian" belief system imaginable, even to the point of clear and unquestionably false doctrine being ministered in the name of Christ under the guise of Christianity. Jesus' prayer was for the unity of all believers, them who make up the collective group of those who confess Jesus as Messiah and follow Him. Every denomination has believers who have accepted Jesus as their Messiah, having been born into a new life as a new creation and there are those who say they are Christians but their lives do not reflect their confession. This mixing of people is not the Church, or Body of Christ, but the church as a social gathering of people in a common place. Jesus refers to this mixture many times through the four Gospels as the wheat and the tare, goat and sheep, and virgin bridesmaids.

Division is seen here both in the meaning of Church and church and within the church. As Jesus prayed for the unity of all believers, the Church, His prayer is continually being answered when people's actions reflect their confession of faith. The Church are the sheep, we are the wheat and the bridesmaids who have their lamps filled with oil. We are the good servants who use the gifts and abilities that God gave us for the advancement of His Kingdom. Herein lays yet another division between the Church and the church.

Socially, the secular church is divided and wars are fought over who is right and who is wrong. The Catholic and Protestant wars of the middle Ages were born from disunity and division in the church, or the social gatherings. The various Crusades for Jerusalem against the Muslims came from this right or wrong mentality, as the Catholic Church felt it was their duty to reclaim Jerusalem from the Muslims through bloodshed. History bears witness to the madness of men over religious ideology. Man is convinced that their outward displays are what please God while their inward intents and actions are indifferent to Him. Man's system is one of self glorification and exaltation while displaying an outward sense of religion to an external deity. Paul describes this condition as "having a form of Godliness but denying the power thereof". Jesus said about the religious leaders of His day that they were "white washed tombs with dead man's bones inside". These are those who serve God with outward displays but without a pure heart before God. These are those who are two faced, whose words and deeds do not reflect the true intent in their hearts. James says it best when he wrote, "faith without works is dead". The same is true in reverse, works without faith is equally as dead, and can be summed up by the word, religiosity.

Religion, when employed as faith and works, becomes worship before God. When we walk day to day according to scripture, we please God and accomplish His will in our lives. As God's Word, or the Bible, is His will, when we daily walk according to His Word, then we are living our lives in accordance to His will. A person who has accepted Jesus as Messiah, repented of their sins, and who has been baptized in Jesus Name, who live their lives in line with scripture has perfect religion. One without the other is only religiosity, a condition not in line with the will of God. Religiosity has shed more blood throughout history than any other conflict of man. The first murder, Cain killing Abel in the Book of Genesis, was committed out of Cain's jealousy of his brother Abel because Abel's sacrifice was accepted by God and his was not. Abel demonstrated perfect religion because he gave his first fruit, his best, to God out of a clean and honest heart. Abel's intentions were pure before God. Cain, on the other hand, did not give his best to God and his intentions were not pure thus showing the first instance of religiosity. Religiosity gives room for sin whereas perfect religion leaves no place for sin in a person's intent. A pure heart before God seeks relationship with Him and shuns any sinful act of their old nature.

The Church is true believers who worship God "in spirit and in truth". Their intentions are pure before God and their action reflect their hearts desire to do things that please God. The Church is "known by the fruit they bear". Paul describes these spiritual fruits in his letter to the Galatians 5:22-23, "but the fruit of the Spirit is love, joy, peace, patience, kindness, goodness, faith, gentleness, self-control. Against such things there is no law". This list of characteristic traits grows in the believer as they grow in their walk with Jesus and in their relationship with Him.

There is a saying, "grow where you are planted". This is a good term to describe the Body of Christ and the evolution of the individual Christian from secularized to sanctified. The message of salvation through Jesus' sacrifice is planted as a seed into the soil of our hearts. Within that seed is life. When a person is humbled, believes in Jesus as Messiah and confesses their sins, that seed is watered by the Holy Spirit and begins to grow into a new life. During a new believer's initial indoctrination into the Christian faith and lifestyle, that seed takes root and begins to break from the soil into the sunlight. As the believer grows stronger, they eventually begin to grow fruit. Some good spiritual fruits are produced, as described by Paul in Galatians and some rotten fruits as well that identify with their dead sinful nature. God prunes these dead, rotten fruit branches in us as we continue to grow into bigger, stronger plants. Then, one day, you become a massive tree, having been through many pruning sessions, or seasons, with God and your good fruits multiply from a few good pieces to the whole batch of all good fruits, or good character traits and actions. Our roots are so firmly planted in good soil and being feed in the waters of the Holy Spirit in that soil that the storms which once blew the small plant all over the place now barely shakes the branches. This is a metaphor for the growth and development of the new born Christian into a mature, older Christian. Just like a baby grows over the years into an adult, Christian growth is an ongoing process, the process of sanctification.

Chapter 11

Spiritual Warfare

References: 2 Corinthians 10:4-6, 1 John 2:16, Romans 7:25, 1 John 5:19, 2 Corinthians 4:4, Colossians 1:13;27, Galatians 5:23-24, Colossians 2:11, Colossians 2:13, Philippians 3:3, Romans 6:6, Galatians 5:17, Galatians 5:19-21, Luke 4:5-8, Revelations 22:20

War is a conflict of wills between two or more opposing forces. Regardless of why a war breaks out, it is defined by violence and death. I have spent a year and six months in Afghanistan as a combatant during Operation Enduring Freedom. During my time there, I became acquainted with violence and the results of that violence. Many Americans are combat veterans and know what I am talking about. These conflicts, no matter what a person's role, are all experienced from different perspectives depending on your mission. Spiritual warfare is the same, in that it is a violent clash of wills between the Kingdom of God and the kingdom of Satan. The main difference is that every believing Christian is on the front lines actively combating the enemy on a daily basis.

We all have a common enemy which we fight daily in life. In Afghanistan, that enemy was the Taliban and AL-Qaeda. Spiritual battles are fought against three enemies, all with the same goal: the flesh (our natural sinful state), the world (this age), and the Devil. Each of these three enemies is out to destroy our walk with God and is at constant battle within our lives.

Our very own nature is to rebel against God before we came to the knowledge of faith and salvation. Even after we are saved, we battle everyday to "crucify our flesh and its desires" as Paul puts it in his letter to the Romans. Paul lists out the characteristic traits of this enemy in Galatians 5:19-21 as sexual immorality, moral impurity, promiscuity, idolatry, sorcery, hatred, strife, jealousy, outbursts of anger, selfish ambitions, dissention, factions, envy, drunkenness, carousing, and similar things. These traits are self seeking and against the Laws of God. They are a part of our fallen, sinful nature; these are the acts and deeds which are inherent in our nature due to Adam and Eve's fall in the Garden of Eden. These traits are what every human being deals with and what separates us from God, even if we are good people in our own understanding prior to receiving Jesus as Lord and Savior. As God's Holy standard is perfection, this natural inclination to sin is directly linked to the sacrifice of Jesus, to bridge the gap between God and man caused by man's fall in the garden. This enemy is a constant and vicious foe not to be underestimated. Many times, Christians blame their problems on the Devil when reality proves that our troubles are the work of our own sinful, human nature.

The second enemy is the world. Scripture mentions the world in two contexts, the first being the planet where we live and the second being the age in which we live in. The Greek word for our enemy is cosmos, which is translated age. Satan is called the "ruler of this age" in John 12:31 by Jesus. The world, or age, is characterized by the varying and changing social, economic, materialistic, and religious philosophies which have their expressions through the organizations and personalities of human beings. This world system is, in its function, a complex, composite expression of the depravity of man and the intrigues of Satan's rule, combining in opposition to the Sovereign rule of God. The world is an extension of the flesh and Satan in that it surrounds man and intensifies our fallen nature. Satan uses the world to question God's Word and through temptation, which is his weapon of choice. The world tempts us to gain its treasures, seeks its approval, gain its power, position, and its honor. The world exalts its own intellectual system and tempts us to reject Christ and tries to dictate our values and tempts believers to conformity. We can see this enemy at work every day in the news when we read about the various political debates that rage around us concerning abortion, homosexuality, and the suppression of Christian morals and values.

The third enemy is Satan and his agents. This is the realm of spiritual warfare where people are in direct contact with demons. Demons are fallen angels who left their proper domain in Heaven when they joined forces with Lucifer, now known as Satan, in his rebellion against God. They were cast to the earth and took on the nature of Satan. The word Satan in the original Hebrew translation means "the accuser". It is Satan who accuses us of sin when we give into temptation. Demons take out their anger and hatred against God through humanity, as we are God's beloved creation whom He loves. Satan attacks our free will through temptation towards sin, which serves to increase our natural inclination towards sin and creates separation between God and us. Because of our free will, we can choose to serve God or Satan. There is no middle ground in this battle, as it is either God or Satan.

There are three main types of demonic activity that a person may face. Many other experts in the field of spiritual warfare go deeper into detail about the levels of demonic activity, but for the sake of a basic understanding of spiritual warfare, I will only mention three commonly agreed methods demons use: infestation, oppression, and possession, better known as demonization.

Demonic infestation is where a home or person is infested with demonic spirits. Much like an insect infestation, demons are all over a person or place. This can occur when a person moves into a residence that is already infested with demons, through a person opening themselves up to demons through occult practices such as séances, Ouija board use, tarot card readings, use of psychics, necromancy, practice in both black and so called white magic (all magic is the domain of Satan), witchcraft, and so forth, or as a result of a curse placed on an individual. In order to have access to a person, a demon must have a legal right through a person's own free will or through Divine permission. Just as God would not remove the "thorn" in Paul's side in 2 Corinthians 12:7-9 but left it there to show Paul that he must rely on God's strength in his weakness, so too we must rely on God's strength in these cases. Through participation in ungodly things, like the examples above, a person gives their permission for a demonic spirit to attach itself to them. Whether it is intentional or not, the person has allowed themselves to become a potential target for demonic infestation. Even being present when other people are playing with Ouija board gives permission because the person is letting the game progress without intervention.

The goal of the infestation is to trick the individual to open up more to the spirit. Demons take the form of people, popularly known as ghosts. This increases the awareness of the spirit, increases interaction with it, and allows the spirit to have greater access to the person's life. Some of the phenomena associated with demonic infestation are hearing tapping or knocking on walls, windows, doors, ect, hearing footsteps, disembodied human voices that might or might not be recognizable to the individual, hearing animal sounds such as grunting, growling, bird noises, and such, smelling offensive odors, seeing so called shadow people, seeing black mist or clouds, and disturbances in electrical devices, such as a digital clock running backwards, as well as lights and appliances turning off and on. Some of these things could very well have a natural explanation and need to be investigated by a Church sanctioned paranormal investigation team, such as North American Demonic Paranormal based out of Raleigh, NC led by David Scott, who is one of only a few Religious Demonologists under the authority of the Church. Having a trained, Church headed team can gather the required evidence needed for Church intervention into a case as well as to debunk anything that may be a natural cause for phenomenon. Most importantly, a team under the authority of the Church goes into a place prepared for spiritual battle in the authority of Jesus Christ and the Church, which is the difference between a team under the Church's authority and other paranormal teams. With that said, a team should only be called in when there is the possibility of demonic activity and any natural explanation is ruled out by the homeowner.

Demonic oppression is the next level of spiritual attack that the diabolical employs against humanity. After a demonic spirit establishes a foothold in a person's life through infestation and the person's will falters, the demon begins oppressing. At this point, the demon begins to affect the individual's emotions and thoughts. The person begins to lose sleep and they begin to hear voices in their head telling them negative, harmful things. There is a distortion of perception as well, especially regarding things such as God, Jesus, the cross, and Church. The victim also begins to see things as well as being scratched, touched, being bitten, as well as other, more graphic forms of touching being reported. It is at this stage that the possibility of a serious mental disorder needs to be ruled out. The Catholic Church, for example, relies heavily on medical expertise from licensed, practicing psychologists, psychiatrist, and medical doctors before considering any diabolical explanation. This form of attack on the individual is designed to wear down the will of the victim until they give into complete control by the demonic spirit. The victim usually begins to feel that they are crazy and the people in their lives, who are unaware of the situation, also have a tendency to believe they are psychotic. The Catholic approach is a fantastic counter to this because, if there is a psychotic explanation, it is properly diagnosed and treated as is the spiritual aspect. Instead of seeing demons behind every tree, any natural explanation is ruled out. Demonic oppression leads to becoming possessed or rather demonized.

The last stage of demonic attack is possession or demonization. When people hear about possession, their imaginations take them to William Freidkin's The Exorcist, featuring a young Linda Blair disfigured, vomiting pea soup and spinning her head 360 degrees. Though this movie was inspired by the book written by William Peter Blatty, which was in turn inspired by true events in the late 40's in St. Louis, theatrics were used to boost ticket sales at the box office, yet reality is more disturbing than what Hollywood can attempt to portray. When a person is demonized, the demon has a much fuller control of the victim's thoughts, emotions, and behavior. They are frequently under the control of the indwelling demon, who talks to them, ordering them what to do with threats of harm if the victim does not comply to the demon's demands. For the victim, it is not easy to ask for help because of threats of harm if the person asks for help and for the physical and mental punishment that results from seeking help. The victim feels abandoned because they cannot easily ask for help, abandoned by family, friends, but especially abandoned by God. These negative feelings allows the demonic spirit to sink it's talons in deeper. For Catholics, a Church Exorcist would be called in to perform the Roman Rite of Exorcism. The Rite is portrayed in many motion pictures that deal with possession. An exorcism can last a day, weeks, months, or even years before the demon is expelled. In the Protestant faith, there are deliverance ministries, though there is no official training, title, or billet held like in the Catholic Church for the most part. Once again, the deliverance can take some time to accomplish depending on the severity of the indwelling as well as the number of demons present.

Perfect demonic possession is very rare. This condition is when the indwelling spirit has total control of its victim at all time. The victim's will has totally broken and they have come to rely on the demon's presence on a psychological level. Perfectly possessed people are unwilling to defy the demons, reject the demon's presence, or renounce their willingness to have the demons possession. Because of this, the victim cannot be freed from the demon's grasp. It is the will of the individual which grants or rejects a demon's authority to be there. God will not violate our will, as love does not do that. Therefore, if a person chooses in their own will to hold onto the demon or demons which possess them, God respects their decision.

Demonized individuals are only under control of the demonic entity on occasion. Demonization is a much more common condition than what is realized. Many times, people suffering from mental conditions that are only getting worse with treatment are demonized. Prayers of deliverance have been known to bring these people relief and discharge from the treatment centers they are admitted in. Because the scientific community does not recognize spiritual matters, the possibility of demonization is not a part of their diagnosis. Over the years, many psychiatrists and psychologists have being awakened to the reality of demonic activity as they are confronted with demons in their work. Many times, psychotic individuals are unaware of their psychosis while demonized individuals are often times aware of a separate entity dwelling within them. While they are under the demon's control, their experience is like a very real nightmare they cannot awake from and sometimes those moments are blank spots in the memory. No matter the experience of the individual while being demonized, they are aware of the demon in their times of lucidity.

I would like to highlight how modern mainstream Protestantism and Church leadership has increasingly forsaken the truths of scripture and spiritual warfare by embracing the lie that demons are metaphors. These false teachers preach that hell is the fallen state of the earth, that Islam and Christianity are compatible and teach essentially the same message, that all people will eventually be allowed into heaven, and that all religious figures in history point to us the way to God. These teachings are apostate and in complete contradiction to the Truth, yet this is the warfare that the enemy is bringing against the body of Christ today, trying to convince us that he does not exist. People under demonic attack, whether through infestation, oppression, or demonization, are increasingly being turned away from their Church leaders because the shepherds do not believe that wolfs exist. Just like sheep, many church goers blindly follow their shepherd. Jesus describes these so called Christian leaders in Matthew 15:14 as "blind leaders of the blind".

A warrior without armor, weapons, and a battle plan is useless in physical and spiritual war. Having the appropriate means to defend and attack is imperative to victory in battle. For our sake, Paul lists the weapons of our warfare in Ephesians 6:11-18. These are truth, righteousness, peace, faith, salvation, the Word of God (scripture), and prayer. It is through the daily implementation of these weapons that we are able to fight against our flesh, the world's system, and demonic attack.

-Truth: being honest and not lying in our daily interactions. The greatest Truth of all, Jesus Christ!

-Righteousness: Though our righteousness is as filthy rags, we accept the righteousness of Christ and walk in accord to the Ten Commandments, which is our standard of living and how we can know sin and avoid it.

-Peace: Living in peace with our fellow man. Not being quarrelsome, but striving to maintain peace in our daily lives.

-Faith: This is faith in the Lord Jesus Christ, that we are redeemed through His sacrificial blood. It is our daily confession of our dependency on God, which is humility. Faith comes by hearing the Word of God.

-Salvation: Salvation is when a person believes in Jesus as the Son of God, who bled and died on the cross for their sins, and was resurrected on the third day. Salvation is trusting in Jesus for your own salvation from death and hell and the confession of that trust.

-Word of God: The written Word of God is the Holy Bible. The Bible is the inspired word of God, written by man under the influence of the Holy Spirit reflecting the will of God. Daily scripture reading and memorization is the main offensive weapon in our battles and is sharper than a double edged sword. Without a means to go on the offensive against an enemy, a soldier can only defend until they are overwhelmed. Scripture is our sword, which discerns the thoughts and intents of our hearts and pierces to the dividing of soul and spirit. Together with prayer, the Word of God is our means of offensive war.

-Prayer: A Christian's life should consist of daily prayer as this is the way in which we communicate between ourselves and God. Like any relationship, communication is the key. Praying before meals and at bed time, though not bad, is not what is going to strengthen your walk with God. Paul tells us to pray for one another with all supplications and to always pray in the spirit. It is this selfless prayer where our compassion, love, and caring of others is developed.

With these weapons and armor, we are able to stand in the evil day against all the devil can throw at us. We can battle our fleshly desires and passions that are inherent in our fallen, human state and crucify them daily. The world's system can hold no sway over us as we seek God's approval instead of the worlds. We become mighty warriors in God and can cast down every strong hold in our lives, overthrowing arguments and everything high thing that rises against Christ in our lives. Every thought we have can be made captive by the weapons of our warfare to Christ Jesus. Daily, we must don the armor and weapons we have been given and fight for the advancement of the Kingdom of God in Jesus Name!

In our spiritual battles, there is no quarter given and no mercy shown to us by our foe. Our enemy is out to steal, kill, and destroy our families, our finances, our jobs, and our walk with Christ. The enemy does not fight fair. If we, as the Body of Christ, choose not to engage in combat against the flesh, the world, and Satan, we become pacifistic. Pacifism has seen the triumph of political correctness in America. When teachers are not allowed to participate in Fellowship of Christian Athletes meetings and coaches are not allowed to bow their heads in respect for the prayers of a player, pacifism is winning out. As our Christian values and moral standards are snubbed out in the name of "religious tolerance", pacifism is winning out. When gay marriage is condoned and homosexuals ministering in the pulpit become acceptable, pacifism has won out. As the Church grows increasingly quiet in fear of being politically incorrect and of losing members of the congregation, pacifism is winning out.

We must stop looking to other people for action and step out in faith. Spiritual war is a battle for the individual, not the collective. The fact is, your Pastor cannot fight your battles. Fellow Christians can fight beside you, but you must make the decision to fight as well. When the individual falls, the collective suffer. Just as a ceiling will fall if enough pillars are removed, so too the collective Body of Christ is weakened as individual Christians choose pacifism over action. Today, as you read this, the choice is yours. Its life and death now, make a choice; whose side are you on? Take up the armor and weapons you have been equipped with and be victorious in your battles in Jesus Name!

Summary

*M*any things can be said both negative and positive about Christians in the world today but none of it matters unless it is directly linked with you. A person cannot make it into heaven based on the salvation of others, but on their own trust in Jesus. We will all stand before God and give account of our every action, thought, intention, and service one of these days. From a person's most well kept secrets to their most personal experience, all will be bare before God. These few basic principles of the Christian faith are the foundations by which a person can build their relationship with God and grow in faith that they might be able to stand before Almighty God proud of their reasonable Christian lives.

From the very first chapter until the last, the basics of the Christian faith have been briefly touched. Like an iceberg bobbing up and down in the water, what you have read is only a small portion of the basics. Every Christian is in a continual state of learning the Word of God, as it is a living Word that holds complexity and simplicity all in one verse. As we learn, we become stronger in the Word and in God's will for our lives.

One of the best things that a Christian can do is to form friendships with other believers. But more than this, establish a relationship that fosters spiritual growth, nourishment, advancement. Proverbs 27:17 tells us "just as iron sharpens iron, so one person sharpens another."

The intent of this book was to illuminate certain aspects of Christianity whereby a person may glean some understanding of the basics. It is an unfortunate thing that many Churches these days do not have any programs geared towards indoctrination into the faith. This book is, as Peter says in 1Peter 2:2, the milk of the Word which will provide for growth into the meat of the Word. Sunday morning services can be confusing to a new believer when they do not grasp the basics of what they are born again into. It is because of this unfortunate reality that I write this short book, as a tool to assist the various ministries across this nation in helping new converts to understand the bare basics of Christianity without the trappings of denominational differences. My hope is that I have accomplished that mission in a respectable and honorable manner that reflects the Glory of God and the Majesty of Jesus Christ for without that, these are just words. May the love of God through Christ Jesus and the Blessings of the Lord always be upon you, may you know the breadth, width, height, and depth of His love for you, may God's Divine presence always surround you, and may you go forth in the knowledge that you are the apple of God's eye, a royal priesthood, a chosen person created for good works, and a mighty warrior in Christ Jesus Name!

"If not now, when? If not me, who? There will never be another today to serve the Lord."

A Moment Of Personal Reflection And Answering The Call

HAVE YOU ACCEPTED JESUS CHRIST IN YOUR LIFE AS LORD AND SAVIOR? HAVE YOU BEEN FORGIVEN OF YOUR SINS BY PLACING YOUR TRUST IN JESUS' SACRIFICE FOR YOU ON THE CROSS? PERHAPS YOU PICKED UP THIS BOOK TO LEARN A LITTLE BIT ABOUT CHRISTIANITY TRYING TO FIND SOMETHING TO FILL THAT HOLE IN YOUR LIFE. MAYBE YOU HAVE ATTENDED CHURCH YOUR WHOLE LIFE BUT HAVE NEVER SURRENDERED YOUR LIFE TO CHRIST. THERE IS NO BETTER TIME THAN NOW AND NO BETTER PLACE THAN THIS TO ACCEPT THE LORD JESUS CHRIST IN YOUR LIFE AS SAVIOR. IF THAT IS YOU, PRAY THIS PRAYER. IT IS JUST AN OUTLINE AND A GUIDE TO HELP YOU, SO FEEL FREE TO SPEAK WHAT IS IN YOUR HEART:

Lord Jesus, I know that I am in need of a Savior. I know that my own good deeds will not save me but it is your sacrifice for me on the cross where I find salvation. Jesus, I believe that you are the Son of God, that You died on the

85

cross for my sins in my place, I believe that you rose from the dead and are seated at the right hand of God making intercessions for me. Forgive me of all my sins and blot them out in Your blood. At this moment, fill my life with Your love, grace, and mercy. Holy Spirit, I open myself up to you, come and reside within me. Thank you, Lord Jesus, for saving me. In Jesus Name I pray, Amen.

If you have prayed this prayer or something like it, you are now saved by the grace of God through your trust in Jesus Christ! Go out and tell someone about what has happened in your heart. If you do not have a Church that you attend, go out and find a congregation of believers where the Word of God is preached without bias and without compromise. Once there, ask the Pastor to baptize you. I look forward to meeting you in Heaven one day!

PERHAPS YOU ARE READING THIS AND ARE NOT LIVING YOUR LIFE LIKE THE CHRISTIAN YOU CLAIM TO BE. MAYBE SOMEWHERE ALONG THE WAY, YOU WERE HURT OR SCORNED BY A FELLOW BELIEVER AND THIS HAS CAUSED YOU TO GIVE UP TRYING TO LIVE THE CHRISTIAN LIFE. MAYBE YOU FEEL AS IF THE CHURCH IS FULL OF HYPOCRITS AND YOU HAVE RAN FROM GOD AS A RESULT. WHATEVER THE SPECIFIC CAUSE, YOU HAVE BEEN HURT BY FRIENDLY FIRE IN THE CHURCH. IF THAT IS YOU, THOUGH PEOPLE HAVE HURT YOU, GOD IS THERE TO HEAL YOU. WHOEVER OR WHATEVER THE CAUSE YOU GIVE FOR YOUR RETREAT FROM CHRIST, IT HAS TO BE FORGIVEN BY YOU. BROTHER OR SISTER IN CHRIST, IT IS NOT THE ACTIONS OF OTHERS BY WHICH WE JUDGE THE WHOLE BODY. INSTEAD OF LOOKING TO

OTHERS FOR HOW YOU BASE YOUR WALK OF FAITH, LOOK TO GOD THROUGH SCRIPTURE. WE, AS HUMAN BEINGS, CAN ERROR AND CAUSE PAIN TO THOSE AROUND US, WHETHER INTENTIONALLY OR UNINTENTIONALLY. BUT WHERE HUMAN ABILITY FAILS, GOD IS ALWAYS FAITHFUL AND NEVER CHANGES, HE NEVER FAILS. I ENCOURAGE YOU TO ASK FORGIVENESS FOR RUNNING FROM GOD, TO FORGIVE THOSE WHO HAVE HURT YOU, AND PICK UP WHERE YOU LEFT OFF. NO MATTER THE SITUATION, NO MATTER THE CIRCUMSTANCES, GOD IS BIGGER THAN THEM ALL AND WILL SEE YOU THROUGH EVERY STEP OF THE WAY. I HAVE BEEN THERE, I CAN TESTIFY TO THIS TRUTH. MAY THE LOVE AND GRACE OF JESUS CHRIST WRAP AROUND YOU THIS VERY MOMENT AS YOU READ THESE WORDS IN JESUS NAME.

CPSIA information can be obtained at www.ICGtesting.com
Printed in the USA
BVOW010014151112

305505BV00001BC/1/P